THE FUNKY KITCHEN
A COMPILATION OF ONE SOCCER MOM'S FAVORITE TRADITIONAL FOOD TECHNIQUES AND RECIPES

*Dear Ellen,
Wishing you
many healthy
meals!
With love,
Sarica*

SARICA CERNOHOUS
L.Ac., MSTOM, BSBA

The information shared in this book is provided in good will for informational and educational purposes only. The ideas and suggestions contained in this book are not intended as a substitute for appropriate care of a licensed health care practitioner, and the author holds no responsibility for the outcome of the use of the techniques, recipes or suggestions.

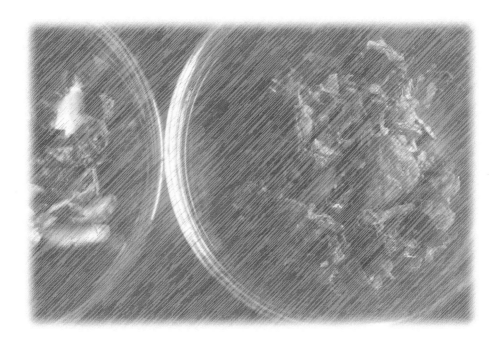

5

★

I would like to thank my incredibly kind and patient husband, Todd, for enduring my learning curves in traditional cooking in the early years of our marriage, and for his unyielding support as I later branched out to share what I'd learned. I don't know how I got so lucky.

I would like to thank my children, Grant and Laurel, for their honest appraisals of my dishes and for having the gumption to try most anything at least once. Thank you for letting Mom get her computer work done!

I would like to thank my parents, Steve and Alice Southerland, for putting up with all my experiments in nutrition over the years. Your leeway helped me to learn through first-hand experience, and sometimes there isn't a better way than that.

I would like to thank my sister, Chef Amy Mirate, who has always been there with answers to my kitchen science questions, and who seems to send on thought-provoking recipes that keep me inspired at all the right times in the kitchen. Thank you so much, Amers—someday I hope to cook as well as you.

I would like to thank my friend, Caron Culbreth, for her excellent direction in copy-editing and suggestions in the early stages of this book—your ideas helped to shape this book profoundly. Many thanks, too, to Linda Shipp and Vera Almann for the incredible makeup and great photos— you are both so talented, and you helped me to bring this book to life.

I would like to thank Dr. Jack Tips, for helping me to see that I might have some ideas that would do well as a book—thank you for your belief in my work and abilities!

This book is dedicated to my grandparents, Gail and LaNelle Southerland, in whose kitchen I found my taste for melted butter and where I always had a place at the table.

TABLE OF CONTENTS

Ancient grains, soaking and fermenting to make delicious bread

Why You Should Read This Book

Thank you for taking an interest in traditional cooking techniques. I believe their use can help all of us find greater vitality through better nutrition. I hope that in this book you will learn the basic components of how to use these invaluable tools, and be inspired to do so.

That being said, these techniques truly do become an art once you understand some of the basic ground-rules…and from that point on, the *terroir* of your cooking environment, encompassing the ingredients you choose to work with, combined with the inherent bacteria and fungal spores in your air, the level of humidity in your cooking space, the seasonings you will select and any derivations on the theme you make to make it your own…all of these pieces will make your kraut different from your neighbor's kraut, your broth different from mine.

So, like any art form, get acquainted with the rules necessary to create your project, then delight in the experience of experimenting and crafting. As you become familiar with the techniques, it is my hope that you will feel your time in the kitchen shift from being one of consumption, to one of creation.

And why might you want to embark on this journey?

First, let's be honest…most people won't make change until their hand is forced to do so. Until someone has been challenged physically with some debilitation, or their child, spouse or some other loved one becomes ill, most people will continue to live their lives as they have been. Of course, there are always exceptions to rules, but my years as a practitioner of alternative, natural medicine have shown me that most people don't make change unless there is a good reason. And when one lives in the land of convenience as most of us do today, it is incredibly easy to buy frozen meals, canned soups, bagged and sliced produce, bottled dressings, pre-packaged lunches for the kids, boxes of cereal, sacks of bread…it is all at our fingertips in our grocery aisles. Technology and innovation have met the demand of more free time from the "drudgery" of kitchen work.

But, what we've gotten in exchange for this convenience has been food of a very different nutrition profile than the foods our great-grandparents consumed. Where our great-grandparents ate raw milk and dairy foods from pastured cows, we consume feed-lot, pasteurized, homogenized milk and dairy products. Where our great-grandparents consumed produce fresh from local farms, preserved by way of lacto-fermentation, cold storage, canning and dehydration, we consume produce picked long-before its peak ripeness, transported and stored until brought to the floors of grocery stores around the country. Where our great-grandparents made porridges, breads and biscuits from scratch, using lard, butter and other simple ingredients, we purchase extruded grain cereals and baked goods, prepared with hydrogenated oils, high fructose corn syrup and fortified with chemically-derived minerals and vitamins.

It wasn't that our forefathers were necessarily thinking they were making better choices…there were no other choices! Similarly, most people today consider that there are only the choices available at their local grocery stores—in their minds, there are no other choices. However, there *are* other choices, and for those who are searching out and using ingredients and methods closer to our ancestors' ways, there can be great benefits to health and vitality.

In an attempt to meet the public demand for quick, easy, palatable, inexpensive foods, many food preparation corners have been cut. These corners are the traditional techniques our ancestors, learned and refined over millennia to enhance the nutrition, reduce the toxicity and improve the flavor of different foods. Without these steps, foods that are common staples in our pantries, refrigerators and freezers can actually be detrimental to our health over time.

However, as many have sought answers to regain their vitality from chronic and debilitating health concerns, there has been a shift in focus from consuming foods of convenience to consuming foods of nourishment. There has been a shift to sourcing nutrient-dense ingredients, and then using traditional food preparation methods to get the most out of those foods. This book will show you many of these basic techniques.

The tools laid out in this book are by no means exhaustive…there are many, many websites, online courses, webinars, e-books and standard texts, and cookbooks to help you grow your experience. I want this book to be a handbook to get you started, and hopefully not leave you feeling overwhelmed. To that end, my suggestion to you is to choose one technique, and keep working with it until you feel very comfortable with it, then move on to something else that piques your fancy.

There's really no right place to begin with all of it. Any move you make will be a big first step in bringing profound nutrition to yourself and your loved ones. There are components in all foods for which science does not yet have names, may not even be aware of their existence. It is these co-factors, these relationships between components, these unnamed healthy bacteria and yeasts…these are the things that have yet to be discovered by science, but which will be found in the foods of your quart-sized glass jars, your crockpot, your dehydrator.

Learning traditional food preparation techniques empowers you in many ways. Even the toughest cuts of meat, the limpest of vegetables, items that you wouldn't otherwise consider edible, all of this and more can find new life and a new expression in these methods. The alchemy of time, proper temperature, acids, beneficial bacteria and yeasts, salt—magic is hewn from these pieces.

And in turn from these efforts, you will no longer be beholden to what is offered on the shelves of your big-box grocery store. While there is plenty that can be done with the offerings found there—dried beans, whole grains, fresh produce, inexpensive bones and cuts of meat—you might very well discover a whole new reason to contact the local farmers in your area for their produce, eggs, meat and dairy.

Not surprisingly, purchasing foods in their more basic forms, unadorned with flavorings and enhancements, will also save money, while at the same time delivering on much deeper nutrition.

Absolutely a win-win! All that is needed is some elbow grease, time and the right ingredients—the rest takes care of itself.

So, join me as we learn together about so much of what has been lost in the modern lifestyle—an appreciation of complex flavors and different textures, of foods that deliver on nutrition better than any designer creations from the lab, of the physical effort and forethought that goes in to truly creating something.

THE IMPORTANCE OF SOURCING GOOD INGREDIENTS FOR THE FOODS YOU PREPARE

Field garlic from our local farmer's Community Supported Agriculture (CSA) offerings

The use of the techniques found in this book will enhance the nutrition of any dishes you create. I read of a woman working with these techniques to support families on very low incomes, showing the families how to ferment canned green beans! Of course, she was doing so, because canned vegetables are a common component of low-income food pantry offerings. Her ingenuity showed how to take a basically inert food (no enzymatic nor bacterial life) and make it live again, through the use of lacto-fermentation, producing something again rich in enzymes, healthy bacteria and various vitamins.

For as wonderful as this example is to exemplify the nutritional power of lacto-fermentation, where we can, it is vitally important that we **do our best to source the highest quality ingredients for our meals**. In my opinion, that means produce that you've either grown yourself, using chemical-free, rich soil, or that you've purchased from a local farmer who uses these methods. This will have you and your loved ones eating foods that are fresh off the vine or stem, full of antioxidants, enzymes, vitamins and minerals. Research has shown that the longer a fruit or vegetable is in transit from picking to consumption, the lower its nutrition value.

Additionally, **eating locally** has us eating foods that are in the correct attunement to the locale and season in which we find ourselves. A quick glance at the offerings at a local farmers' market will reveal foods that are in right keeping with the season in which we consume them...Vitamin C-rich citrus fruits during the cold and flu season of autumn; root vegetables such as yams and sweet potatoes, again, full of Vitamin C and Beta Carotene, supporting the immune system and the vision through the cold, dark days of winter; sprouts and baby greens during the windy, transitional spring, nourishing our bodies in preparation for summer with minerals and chlorophyll; and the luscious, sweet, juicy fruits of summer, rehydrating us from our physical pursuits in the bright, hot sun with their natural sugars and water content.

The scent of fermented foods—even nuts and seeds—is a sign of the predigestion of nutrients by way of beneficial bacteria

Radishes, beet greens, beets and sea salt, in preparation for homemade sauerkraut.

And when these foods are grown locally, these nutritional attributes have an opportunity to develop to their full potential in the plant and the produce it bears, rather than being picked early for ease of transport and shelf life.

It is also incredibly important to **consume foods made from animals that have been reared in their natural environment**. This may seem a reasonable request, but any cursory Google search of "Factory Farming Techniques" will reveal that this is far from the norm of modern food production. To illustrate the changes that occur when animals are moved to different environments and fed different foods, consider the effects of such changes on a common nutrient most are familiar with: Omega-3 fatty acids. And while most of us think we need to consume fatty, cold-water fish, or eggs from hens fed an Omega-3 rich ration, cows reared in their correct habitat, eating the foods they've evolved to consume, can create a rich source of Omega-3 fats as well.

The fatty acid composition of the meat and dairy of cows raised in confinement and fed a grain-based diet (the common practice in the factory farm) is very different than a cow reared on pasture, consuming grass. In fact, research has shown that for every day a pastured, grass-eating cow spends in confinement at the feedlot on a grain diet, the fatty acid profile of their meat, fat and milk changes from Omega-3 dominant to increasingly Omega-6 dominant.

Pastured beef, Celtic sea salt and garden rosemary for bone broth

How does this number change so drastically? Well, just like humans, animals are what they eat. If an herbivore, such as a cow, is consuming predominately grass, it will have a body composition that reflects that. And since the fats in grass are on average 60% Omega-3s, then the cow's tissues will be rich in Omega-3s. And, because corn and other grains from the feedlot are high in Omega-6s, when these animals shift to consuming these foods, so will their bodies' tissues.

Omega-3 fats are essential, meaning our bodies cannot produce them, but are vitally necessary for normal cellular activity. Research has shown their positive effect in various cardiovascular concerns, inflammatory patterns, cognitive development and psychiatric disorders.

Next time you find yourself at the grocery store, look around at your fellow shoppers. Do you see robust people, with baskets full of fresh, organic produce, grass-fed meats, eggs from pastured hens? (Actually, this is an unfair question because most of these foods aren't even available at your standard grocery store, but please play along with the scenario!) Or do you see people who are struggling in some way, with boxes of cold cereal, frozen meals, bags of pasta, canned and jarred produce, conventionally-grown meat, dairy and egg products, filling up their carts?

Again, we are what we eat, and most in modern society are woefully low in Omega-3 fatty acids because of what is eaten. In fact, a study from 1991 showed Omega-3 concentrations in the blood of participants to be undetectable in 20% of those tested! Where might that number be now, with the seemingly never-ending consumption of vegetable oil-laden, Omega-6 dominant, processed foods?

Research suggests that historically humans consumed a 1-to-1 ratio of Omega-6 to Omega-3. In current western diets, this ratio has shifted from about 16-to-1 (and sometimes much higher than that), thanks in large part to the 20th Century explosion of Omega-6 dominant vegetable oils in convenience foods.

Research for yourself—or ask one of your fellow shoppers--about how they're feeling as they consume their basket-full of processed foods. Their answers will tell the story of what research has shown: Omega-6 dominance is associated with various inflammatory processes, from pain to cardiovascular disease, from cancer to autoimmune disease…common maladies in our times.

Thankfully, increasing Omega-3 fats in the diet, bringing the Omega 6-to-Omega 3 ratio closer to its historical balance, has been shown to have incredible health benefits. From decreased mortality in patients diagnosed with cardiovascular disease; to reduced cell proliferation in patients with colon cancer; to decreased risks associated with breast cancer; to reduction of pain and inflammation in those with rheumatoid arthritis; to improvement in asthmatic presentations, a seemingly wide variety of ailments are relieved by something as simple as changing the fat we eat.

There are countless other benefits to the nutritional profile of animals reared in their natural conditions, consuming the foods they've evolved to eat. To read more, please visit EatWild.com for an extensive list of research. But at the very least, remember that consuming the meat, bones, organs, eggs and dairy from animals that have been raised in a proper, healthy environment will make for a **healthier animal that does not require the battery of antibiotics, medications and hormones needed to keep that animal producing and growing**. In turn, this removes the traces of these components from these animal foods you will be consuming—if they were never administered to the animal, then they won't be fed to you.

Homemade, raw cow's milk yogurt

As relates to sourcing grains, beans/legumes, nuts and seeds, **buy these in small batches, spend a little more for organic, make sure they have not been irradiated and store them in a cool, dark place** (a refrigerator or freezer works great) until you are ready to use them. These techniques of traditional food preparation will often rely on ingredients that have a life vitality nestled in them. If nuts, seeds, grains or beans/legumes do not have this life spark (either because they are old and rancid, or because all life activity has been destroyed through irradiation), they will be unable to germinate and sprout. Avoid the open bulk bins at the grocery stores—light and air make for oxidation of the delicate oils in these foods, and many can go rancid quickly in these conditions. Better to buy small, air-tight bags of the foods you'll want to prepare. If you do opt to purchase a larger size, make sure it's fresh to begin with (look at the "Packed On" date), then store any unused portion in a cool, dark place, with as much of the air pushed out of the bag or container as possible.

Dried pinto beans soaking in filtered water and water kefir

There are also various kitchen tools, appliances and other components that will make your experience so much more enjoyable if you have them on hand. While each chapter discusses the tools you'll need for each technique, here is a list that includes all suggestions, and some others:

- 2-Cup Wide Mouth Glass Canning Jars, with lids, 4-6 each
- 1-Quart Wide Mouth Glass Canning Jars, with lids, 4-6 each
- Wooden Spoons for mixing
- Silicone Spatulas for mixing
- Paper towels with rubber bands for cinching (could use cleaned kitchen towels)

- Meat Thermometer for gauging temperature
- Soup Ladle for broth
- Smaller 2-3-Quart Saucepan
- Coffee Grinder for blending dried herbs, reducing the size and density of a small amount of dried grains—just be careful extra hard grains do not cause pieces of the steel blade to chip off and that you don't run it too long which can burn up its small motor
- Larger Stockpot
- 4-5-Quart Dutch Oven for baking
- Pyrex-style Large Glass Mixing/ Serving Bowls
- Fine-mesh Bamboo or Plastic Small Strainer for filtering kefir grains and yogurt curds from whey
- Large Colander to drain beans, grains and produce
- Fine-mesh Small to Medium Stainless Steel Strainer for small grains and beans
- Quality Chef's Knife for slicing and preparing produce and meats
- 2 Wooden or Bamboo cutting boards (1 for meat, 1 for produce)
- Box Grater for shredding produce
- Food Dehydrator with multiple, removable trays (could use oven on lowest setting in lieu of, though the temperatures will be higher)
- 5-6-Quart Crock Pot with adjustable time and/or temperature (could use a large stockpot on the stove, but requires more attention and care)
- Food Processor for pureeing beans, preparing produce, blending dressings (could often use a blender, knife and cutting board, and/or box grater)
- Grain Mill, or Grain Mill Attachment to a food processor (grain mills are much stronger than coffee grinders and a decent mill will not cause excessive heating of the grain as a stainless steel coffee grinder blade can)

AS YOU GET STARTED

You will undoubtedly come to see that there will be some added effort and usually an increase in price for endeavoring to find, purchase and prepare foods that reflect these greater nutritional attributes. However, with the advent of the Internet, refrigerated shipping, farmers' markets, buying clubs and food co-ops, natural foods' stores and many other sources (see *Resources* at the back of this book), it is possible and often quite

21

reasonable to make these changes to your diet and lifestyle. It all requires just a little bit of forethought and advance preparation. It may not be as quick and handy as running into the local convenience store and grabbing a snack, but once you have attuned your palate to fresh flavors and felt the vitality of eating truly nutritious foods, you may very well notice that you come to view such convenience store offerings as you would the gas being sold outside—nothing you would even consider putting in your mouth!

A santé!
Sarica Cernohous, L.Ac., MSTOM, BSBA
Arizona, February 2013

FERMENTED VEGETABLES

Easy-to-make, fun-to-eat homemade fermented vegetables

Homemade, lacto-fermented, raw vegetables are nutrition powerhouses, a bold statement by the forkful, aiding with digestion and adding a unique flavor dimension to a meal.

Fermented vegetables, in all their various incarnations, have been consumed the world over for thousands of years. Here in the west, cabbage-based sauerkraut is what most of us think of as relates to cultured vegetables, but there are countless other variations…*kimchi*, the spicy, bok choy-based condiment of Korea; various Chinese pickling creations, each regionally-influenced and unique to the varying fauna and spices of that diverse country; *kawal* of Darfur; *gundruk* from the Himalayas; salty, brined cucumbers—also known as pickles---in western cuisine; Mediterranean olives soaked and cured in salt water…the list goes on and on.

And of all the ways to bring homemade cultured foods into your kitchen, fermenting vegetables is probably the easiest, least expensive and most forgiving option. Grab your garden gloves and let's dig in!

Vegetables chopped, salted and primed with a culture starter on the left, ready for cool storage. On the right, the same ingredients six weeks later—fermented and ready to enjoy.

A Little on the History of Fermented Vegetables

Fermentation is part of the normal process of vegetable matter decomposition   And somewhere, long ago, someone started harnessing this natural phenomenon to be put to use to make otherwise indigestible plants an edible food (think of the tough, fibrous taro root of Hawaii becoming the pudding-like condiment, *poi*.) It is also a preservation technique of seasonal, regional fresh foods--before the advent of refrigeration or other preservation techniques, this technique literally saved lives (a dramatic example is the means by which Captain Cook prevented scurvy in his ship's crewmen by rationing Vitamin-C rich sauerkraut during long voyages, when nary a live plant was seen for months on the open sea.)

The process of fermentation was likely put to formal use in China, thousands of years ago. In the 1850's, Louis Pasteur of France became the first *zymurgist*, or scientist of fermentation, using microscopes and lab equipment to prove that this magical process was the result of the actions of living cells. In fact, it was Pasteur who devised the method of destroying the activity of microorganisms by high-temperature heating of the foods in which they inherently reside, the process we know today as *pasteurization*.

WHY YOU SHOULD EAT MORE FERMENTED VEGETABLES

Fermented foods truly are nutrition dynamos. It is an interesting thing that happens, when native lacto-bacillus bacteria are given an opportunity to do their work—the environment they create protects the otherwise heat and oxygen-sensitive Vitamin C in plant matter, maintaining it for extended periods; B Vitamins are generated; digestion-supporting enzymes are released; carbohydrates are transformed into acids and simpler sugars; gut-benefiting beneficial bacteria are created in abundance. This short list is anything but exhaustive of the nutrition found in ferments; it really is amazing what those little bacteria can do.

Let's look at these different benefits a little more closely:

- VITAMIN C RETENTION—While lacto-fermentation does not generate new Vitamin C, the process itself helps to maintain the inherent Vitamin C content in the foods that have been fermented. In the fermentation process—which is an anaerobic activity--carbon dioxide (CO_2) is generated (this is the reason for the fizziness of beer and water kefir.) Since Vitamin C is highly reactive to and degraded by oxygen, the anaerobic, CO_2-rich environment has a protective action on this nutrient. It is only after the CO_2 is no longer being generated by the bacteria that Vitamin C begins to slowly degrade. This is in stark contrast to oxidation of Vitamin C in raw, unfermented vegetable matter. Potatoes, a staple source of Vitamin C for the Irish people during the long, cold, grey winter months, may lose 75% of their Vitamin C during 9 months of storage. Vitamin C is a nutrient that is very unstable in the presence of oxygen, and yet it is vital to our body's nutritional requirements. Having a relatively stable source of it is incredibly important for immunity, tissue repair and recovery from oxidative stress.

- **GENERATION OF B VITAMINS**—The fermentation process tends to generate B Vitamins—B1, thiamin; B2, riboflavin; and B3, niacin--even if there were negligible amounts of these vitamins in the raw foods from which the ferment is created. (It should be noted that it was once believed that Vitamin B12 was created by lacto-fermentation, but research has shown that, in fact, this is an inactive B12 analogue that does not exhibit the same functions as true B12.) These B Vitamins are essential for energy production and healthy muscle, nerve, cardiovascular and digestive tissues and activity.

- **ENZYMATIC ACTIVITY**—Our pancreas and liver are largely responsible for much of the enzyme production in our digestive system. Enzymes are catalysts that allow given processes to occur. If a person is eating a diet largely devoid of enzyme-rich foods (anything that is heated over 118°F/48°C, which would constitute most modern, processed foods), then the liver and pancreas must work harder to generate more enzymes to allow for digestion and other life processes. If we can supply foods that are rich in enzymes, such as ferments, then we are inherently lightening the load on our systems.

- **CARBOHYDRATE BREAKDOWN**—Lactic acid bacteria and some beneficial yeasts consume various carbohydrates in the foods being fermented, creating in the wake of this transformation lactic acid, acetic acid and carbon dioxide. Because this is an anaerobic process, it generates an acidic environment that is inhospitable to many dangerous aerobic bacteria such as *pseudomonas* and *acinetobacter* species. This makes these foods low in pancreas-taxing carbohydrates as well as very safe.

- **HEALTHY BACTERIA**—As mentioned, lacto-fermented foods can be full of beneficial bacteria and yeasts (a.k.a., probiotics, what many of us pay for in capsule and liquid forms at the natural foods' store.) The degree to which lab-created probiotics have benefited our health has been borne out by research; however, the manner in which this benefit occurs is not as clear. Given that there are numerous pH gradients, tissue differences, enzymatic influences and microbiome variances throughout the digestive tract, it is not surprising that this aspect of beneficial bacteria ingestion is not well understood. And while there is not the degree of funding for the beneficial effects of lacto-fermented foods that there is for lab-created, industry-sponsored probiotics, there has been benefit shown in various research projects. However, as with probiotics in a capsule, if the fermented foods are then heated above 115°F/46°C, then this benefit is lost.

HOW WE USE FERMENTED VEGETABLES IN OUR KITCHEN

I like to create vegetable ferments from what is growing prolifically in either our local farmer's garden, or in the raised growing beds in our backyard. I have a couple of favorite techniques. One is natural or wild fermentation, where I'll lean on the native lactic acid-producing bacteria on the vegetables, which come to life when the juices and enzymes of the vegetables have been released through the chopping, squeezing, shredding and/or salting that occurs when preparing them for sauerkraut or brining. The other option is to use a little bit of a starter—maybe the whey from homemade yogurt, or a few tablespoons of water kefir—to hasten the fermentation process a little more quickly, giving it some direction.   Both options have worked beautifully.

SOME CONSIDERATIONS

- Remember, lacto-fermentation is an anaerobic activity. Therefore, it is key that there are **no air pockets** down in your ferment—press all ingredients down tightly to keep all air out below. And make sure your **ingredients are under the liquid of the ferment**. Anything exposed to air has the potential to form mold, or at the very least oxidize. If white mold forms, it is probably best to throw away all of the ferment. While many fermenters believe that simply scooping the mold away is sufficient, **the naked eye cannot discern any of the roots to the mold that was evidenced at the top of the ferment**. These roots can penetrate all the way down into the vegetables. And while they may not make a person immediately sick (or they might!) they can create a mold-sensitivity or other illnesses down the line.

- To keep the edible part of your ferment submerged under its own liquids and kept from oxidizing, you may choose to use some kind of a weight. Tightly rolled cabbage, beet, chard or kale leaves work great. Simply roll each leaf tightly and set them side by side, like sardines in a tin. Make the layer of leaves deep enough so that all the ferment's ingredients are submerged under the liquid, with the leaves being pushed down by the lid of the jar. This is a great option for brining looser ingredients, where their tendency is to float to the top of the liquid. The next simple step is to pour over the top of all the vegetables a ¼"- ½" layer of olive oil. The olive oil will create an air-tight barrier that allows the gasses from the carbon dioxide (CO_2) production to be released, without allowing any of the oxygen at the top of the jar to react with the vegetables.

- During the process of fermentation, a lot of CO_2 may be generated, so you might gently release a little of the carbonation pressure every few days to keep the ferment from bubbling up and out of the tightly closed jar. Working with a glass jar with a twist-on lid allows for a little pressure releasing from time to time. Or, you can just place your jars in a baking dish to catch any juices that might spill over during the fermentation process.

Opening a jar of beet and bok choy sauerkraut that had been fermenting in the cupboard for six weeks. Best to do this over the sink, as there is often a lot of liquid that rushes to the top, not unlike opening a champagne bottle!

- The longer you allow fermentation to occur, the more the bacterial profile, flavor and consistency changes. A small ferment (as these recipes will be), kept at comfortable room temperatures (62°-72°F/ 17°-22°C), can first be consumed as early as after seven days of production. **However, for the most gut-healing benefit from development of new strains of beneficial bacteria, it is best to allow at least four weeks of fermentation.**

- If you wish to ferment longer, and you want to keep the crunchiness of the vegetables intact, use a little more salt than what is called for in these suggestions—maybe a tablespoons' worth. Also, avoid cucumbers and the soft-fleshed summer squashes if you're wishing to avoid a soggier texture.

- Use organic and preferably local produce—this will give you the most nutrition and the greatest flavor.

- Warmer temperatures will hasten the fermentation process—higher heat makes for more active microbes. If it's the middle of summer and your fermenting spot is above 72°F/22°C or so, look for a cooler spot, such as the lowest shelf at the back of a dark pantry, or an ice chest stored in a cool area of the house with one or two ice packs switched out every day or so. Likewise, overly cool temperatures, in the range of 50°F/10°C and below, will slow the fermentation process. This isn't a huge concern if you're planning to leave your ferment for a few months before consuming, but if you're wishing to enjoy it within a a week to four weeks (which is the design of these recipes), then store it at temperatures closer to comfortable room temperature, in the mid-60's to low 70's. For a very cool house, such a warm spot might be found on top of a refrigerator or some other high spot, where rising heat will make the air temperature warmer than below. Also, using an ice chest, in which a couple of bottles of hot water have been stored, can create a warmer environment.

- While any salt will work when fermenting, please opt for a minimally-processed sea salt (I like Celtic, Hawaiian red and pink Himalayan sea salts, in which you can see the color of the mineral content.)

The whitish-grey crystals are Celtic sea salt, and the amber-tinted are Hawaiian Red sea salt crystals.

- Most people use vegetables of the cruciferous, *Brassica* family when making ferments. While these foods have many nutritional benefits, they all have a compound in them that impedes thyroid function when taken in raw and/or fermented form. Known as *goitrogens*, these components block various aspects of thyroid hormone production and use. If you know you have impaired thyroid function, then you may want to limit your consumption and use of these foods in the raw or fermented states. Bok choy, cabbage, broccoli, cauliflower, mustard greens and turnips are some of the more common brassica family vegetables.

Some examples of non-brassica ingredients…red bell pepper and beet roots and leaves

- Do not feel beholden to the ingredients I've used below—fermentation of vegetables is only as limited as the fresh options you have available. Use what is offered at your farmer's market, or what is popping out of your own garden. Brining lends itself toward preservation of any number of vegetables and vegetable-like fruits, as well as fresh beans. Try your hand at brining sliced cucumbers with lemon rind, quarter-sized hot peppers with carrots, or green beans with garlic and dill—have fun and enjoy! Don't hesitate to use the Internet—people love sharing their homemade successes with vegetable fermentation.

- When opting to brine for fermentation, use filtered, chlorine-free water. Chlorine can weaken and destroy the beneficial bacteria. If your water contains chlorine, pour the water into a carafe to air out for a day before using in the brine.

Fresh veggies to ferment on the left; same ingredients 6 weeks later, post-fermentation

Sauerkraut in a Jar

Homemade sauerkraut—the magenta coloration comes from fresh beets

Makes approximately 2 quarts
- 1 medium-sized head of Green or Purple Cabbage, rinsed (approximately 4 cups raw and shredded)
- 1 bunch Rainbow Chard leaves, rinsed well and ends trimmed (approximately 3-4 cups raw and finely chopped)
- 3 large Carrots, scrubbed well (approximately 2 cups, shredded)
- 2 small Beets, scrubbed well (approximately 1 cup, shredded)
- 3 Yellow, Orange and/or Red Bell Pepper, rinsed and seeded (approximately 3 cups, chopped)
- 2-3 medium Summer Squash (Yellow Crookneck, Zucchini, or Pattypan), rinsed and tips removed (approximately 1-2 cups , shredded)

- 1 large Purple Onion (a little over a cup, chopped)
- 4-5 tablespoons Sea Salt
- 2-3 tablespoons of fresh Whey or Water Kefir (not necessary, but makes this otherwise wild ferment a cultured ferment, giving it clear direction on the types of bacteria to propagate)
- ¼ - ½ cup Organic Olive Oil, to top the vegetables and act as a barrier to oxygenation

Optional, for flavor and nutrition variation:
- 1 bunch Cilantro, rinsed and ends trimmed (approximately ¾ cup, chopped)
- 3-4 cloves Garlic (approximately 3-4 tablespoons, chopped)
- 1 bunch Italian Parsley, rinsed and ends trimmed (approximately 1 cup, chopped)
- 1-2 Hot Peppers, such as Habanero or Jalapeno (approximately 2 tablespoons, finely chopped—remove seeds if you want a milder version)
- 1 Lemon or Lime, rinsed well and tips removed (approximately ½ cup, including the rind, sliced very thinly)
- 2-3 pieces of rehydrated Seaweed, such as Kombu or Wakame (soak dried seaweed in water for 10 minutes, then chop finely) Seaweed will increase iodine and other trace minerals, vital for thyroid support
- Additional vegetable leaves to be used as a wedge to prevent oxidation, if you choose

METHOD

As you finish preparing each of the ingredients, place them in a large, stainless steel bowl and lightly sprinkle with a little of the 4-5 tablespoons of sea salt, so that the salt is well-incorporated into the vegetables. Additionally, if you're using a culture starter, such as water kefir or fresh whey, pour a little of it in with each successively prepared ingredient. This will help release the vegetables' juices and ensure that the vegetables are well coated in salt and beneficial bacteria.

Sea salt and water kefir to support the fermentation process

Shred the cabbage into thin slices, using either a cutting board and very sharp chef's knife, or the shredding attachment for a food processor (FP). Next thinly slice the chard leaves, including the stems, or use the FP slicing attachment. Shred the carrots and beets, using a grater, or the FP grating attachment. Chop the peppers into coarse pieces, or use the thin slicing FP attachment. Shred the squash with a grater, or use the FP grating attachment. Finely chop the onion, or use the FP grating attachment. Add any other optional ingredients.

Making sauerkraut isn't hard—but it does require elbow grease and patience

Soon, these raw vegetables will be transformed into a juicy mix by way of salt and physical effort

Mix all ingredients and begin squeezing with bare, clean hands, and/or pound, using a meat tenderizer (this method is why I suggest putting all ingredients into a steel bowl! If you're going to simply squeeze the ingredients, then you can use a glass bowl.) Keep squeezing and/or pounding until juices are running freely from the vegetables, with liquid pooling at the bottom of the bowl. If intending to include fresh whey or water kefir, incorporate it at this stage and mix well into the ingredients.

Slicing, shredding, pounding...be sure to wear an apron when making kraut and be mindful of your fingers

While a food processor will reduce much of this work, you'll still need to pound and mix the veggies and salt

Chopped and sliced, ready for pounding and mixing

Adding the salt

Including some water kefir, to prime the mixture with beneficial bacteria. Then, let the pounding and squishing begin!

After a hefty pounding, coupled with salt and water kefir, the juices of the vegetables are flowing freely and will be an integral part of the anaerobic fermentation process

Begin filling two clean glass quart jars with the ingredients, pressing down hard with each scoop to remove any air pockets. You should have enough vegetables to fill each jar to about an inch or two shy of the top. If you have extra, you can place it in a smaller glass jar to ferment, or you can enjoy it immediately as a salad topper or sandwich filler. If there is a lot of space left at the top of the jars, you can use smaller jars that will better accommodate the quantity you've created.

Press the ingredients down hard, so that they are totally submerged under their own liquid. It is not a problem if a few pieces of them float to the top—this amount will likely oxidize and just need to be removed before consuming. If you don't want this to occur, then use the method of rolling vegetable leaves as outlined in the *Considerations* section above, and cover everything with a healthy layer of olive oil, so that everything is under at least ¼ - ½ inch of oil.

Compressing the vegetables really tightly into the jar and rolling beet leaves to keep the kraut submerged under its own liquids. I next pour ¼ - ½ cup of olive oil over the top to create an airtight layer to prevent mold formation.

Close the jars with a standard lid and place them in your cupboard to be kept at cool room temperatures (55°-72°F/13°-22°C.) In case the CO2 generated by the fermentation process causes the liquids to push out the top of the covered jars, consider placing them in a shallow baking dish to catch any spills.

You can begin enjoying the vegetables as soon as seven days later, though much greater beneficial bacteria will be created if you leave them for at least 30 days. If you used vegetable leaves for compression, covered with a layer of olive oil, gently pour off the oil, and you can either consume the vegetable leaves or discard them. Store, covered, in the refrigerator to significantly slow the fermentation process.

Serve as a condiment to sandwiches, as an accompaniment to meats and as a topper to soups and salads. Of course, you can certainly just enjoy a spoonful by itself!

BRINED RADISHES

Radishes from our winter garden

MAKES APPROXIMATELY 2 CUPS
- 1 large bunch of Radishes, rinsed well and ends trimmed (approximately 1-1.5 cups sliced)
- 1 cup purified, chlorine-free Water
- 1 tablespoon Sea Salt, dissolved into ¼ cup very warm water
- 1 clove Garlic, finely minced (approximately ½ teaspoon)
- ¼ teaspoon dried Oregano
- ¼ teaspoon dried Basil
- 1 tablespoon fresh Whey or Water Kefir, if you choose
- Additional vegetable leaves to be used as a wedge to prevent oxidation from radishes floating to the top during the fermentation process

- ¼ - ½ cup Organic Olive Oil to act as a top barrier against mold and oxygentation

METHOD

Slice the radishes into quarter-sized rounds, about 1/8 inch thick. Place in a 2-cup glass jar, adding the garlic and herbs. Pour over the water and salt water.

Tightly roll vegetable leaves and place over the top of the ingredients, creating a wedge to keep the radishes submerged below the liquid. Pour over a ¼ - ½ inch layer of olive oil, covering the rolled leaves. Cover tightly and store for at least three days in a room-temperature cupboard, though a month's time will deliver on more beneficial bacteria. When you are ready to enjoy them, carefully pour off the oil and discard the rolled leaves. Transfer to the refrigerator to significantly slow the culturing process. These are excellent as a condiment with meats, or as an addition to sandwiches and wraps. They're a delightful little snack in their own right, as well.

BONE BROTH

Rosemary and pastured beef shanks in the crockpot

Bone broth is possibly one of the most nutritious components in the traditional food compendium. As such, you'll notice that I've given a little more on the research supporting its benefits than I have the other chapters. Hopefully this will inspire you to start using it regularly in your kitchen, and enjoying all the subtle and powerful attributes it offers.

BONE BROTH, A BRIEF HISTORY

Broths have been a key player on the stoves and in the hearths of humanity, dizzying the senses as their aromas envelop the entire home. They add a depth of flavor, that *umami* quality—the pleasant, rich taste—to any recipe.

Whether used to cook grains or beans, or as the base of a soup, or to deepen the flavor of sautéed vegetables, or as a simple, delicious pre-meal appetizer, homemade broth can make all the difference between run-of-the-mill dishes and those that will make you wonder why you would ever want to buy canned soup again.

And broths offer so much more than simple enjoyment; they are an incredibly economical way to get the most nourishment from every last edible part of an animal or vegetable, even making the inedible—onion skins, bones and connective tissues—a flavorful and nutritious part of the broth.

MSG AND BROTHS

Science has done its best to replicate the deep flavor that one finds in a rich broth…we are hard-wired to have our appetites stimulated by the complexity and depth of such a long-simmered food. In 1866, a German chemist, Karl Rotthausen, identified the amino acid that is responsible for this flavor profile: glutamic acid.

In the early 20th Century, Japanese researcher Kikunae Ikeda, after having enjoyed a delicious bowl of his wife's seaweed soup, pondered why it was so flavorful, while not being overly salty, nor too heavily flavored in the other four flavors of sweet, bitter, sour and pungent. He dehydrated the broth and found as its major composition glutamic acid. He coined this flavor profile *umami*, a term that is often described today as the sixth flavor, one that offers complexity and depth to a food. In turn, he developed a product that is used in various forms the world over today to replicate that depth of flavor: MSG.

In its various forms, MSG is truly ubiquitous in the modern food supply. But you might think, "I never see MSG on the labels of the food I'm eating, so it must be the next shopper who's eating it." Unfortunately, it is not so simple. As mentioned, at its base, MSG is glutamic acid. And this amino acid can come in under the guise of many other names, various Trojan Horses to increase the flavor of foods that are otherwise quite lacking in nutrition and flavor complexity. Other ingredients that are or may be* MSG derivatives:

Hidden Forms of MSG and MSG Derivatives

- *Autolyzed yeast*
- *Barley malt**
- *Bouillon**
- *Broth**
- *Calcium caseinate*
- *Carageenan**
- *Enzyme modified ingredients**
- *Fermented ingredients**
- *Gelatin**
- *Glutamate*
- *Glutamic acid*
- *Hydrolyzed corn gluten*
- *Hydrolyzed ingredients*
- *Hydrolyzed protein*
- *Malt extract* & flavorings**
- *Maltodextrin**
- *Monosodium glutamate*
- *Monopotassium glutamate*
- *Natural flavors**
- *Pectin**
- *Protease**
- *Protein fortified ingredients**
- *Seasonings**
- *Sodium caseinate*
- *Soy sauce**
- *Soy protein*, isolate*, concentrate**
- *Stock**
- *Textured vegetable protein*
- *Whey protein*, isolate*, concentrate**
- *Wheat protein*
- *Yeast extract*

- *Yeast food*
- *Yeast nutrient*

(Note: Not all of the additives marked with * are necessarily MSG derivatives. Research the manufacturer of foods listing these ingredients to learn more of the specifics of their sourcing and use in the final product.)

Why should we be concerned with sprinkling a little MSG over a dish, or purchasing a prepared soup or other food flavor-enhanced with MSG?

First, MSG can be quite addictive. It is recognized as an *excitotoxin*, a food that can have damaging consequences for brain and neural tissues. MSG and its derivatives have been linked to obesity, violent and irrational behavior, lesions in the hypothalamus and headaches.

Second, you will be missing out on the nutrition that is part and parcel with a long, slow cooking of bones and connective tissues. Bone broths are saturated with incredible nutrition.

And while the ancient Chinese prescribed broths for recovery from injury and illness, my belief is that most people of this day and age are so physically and mentally taxed, that regular use of a homemade broth is in order. I'm sure if a Chinese doctor of long ago bore witness to the caffeine-consuming, refined-food eating, mega-hour weeks of working, dual-income producing, lack of balanced exercising, not sufficiently-resting modern day human experience we call life, he would feel the same way.

The simple ingredients for a full-flavored, nutrient-dense broth—pastured beef shank, garden rosemary, Celtic salt and raw apple cider vinegar.

WHAT MAKES BROTH SO SPECIAL AND WHY SHOULD YOU EAT IT?

When we look at the composition of a broth, there is so much to love, not the least of which is the amino acid, *glycine*. This incredible nutrient is foundational in these life processes:

- The construction of new protein structures in the body
- The detoxification process
- Proper acid secretion for good digestion
- Wound healing
- A necessary component in the construction of glucose

Clearly, glycine's functions are broad and necessary. But many people today are in dire need of it, especially pregnant women, those consuming low-protein diets, infants and children. And if the body isn't able to make enough of it, then these functions are plainly compromised. Therefore, consuming it in the diet is key.

Unfortunately, most of modern society has stopped consuming one of the greatest sources of glycine: Bone broth. Thankfully, broths are easy to prepare and taste great—who would have thought that wound repair, skin health, muscle tone, detoxification and digestive support could taste so good?

Abundant and easy-to-digest minerals are another benefit to consuming bone broths. By adding a bit of an acid such as apple cider vinegar to the water and bones as they cook, the mineral composition of the bones is leached from their bony structure and infused into the broth solution. Bringing calcium, magnesium, phosphorus and many trace minerals into the liquid makes for a delightfully delicious way to help insure a healthy intake of minerals.

And while many of us think of minerals as relates to our skeletal system, their functions are many in the body. Certainly, they are absolutely essential to healthy bones, but they are foundational in proper adrenal balance, mood regulation, muscle performance and cardiovascular function, to name a few. In other words, if you want a strong physique, abundant energy, happy outlook and a healthy heart to support it all, then make sure you're eating plenty of minerals your body can put to use.

Finally (but by no means the last accolade of bone broths), *the gelatin content of a broth made from the bones of a pastured animal is a very bioavailable means of helping with protein assimilation.* The use of gelatin in recovery from convalescence, when little else can be tolerated, has been demonstrated throughout history. Because gelatin is rich in the afore-mentioned glycine, it soothes disturbed digestive function, which enhances gastric acid secretions. This scenario allows for greater digestibility of all foods, not just the broth.

Generally, the broths richest in gelatin come from feet bones, from pastured poultry, and from wild-caught fish heads and bones. How will you know if your broth is rich in gelatin? If you cool it in the refrigerator, it should gel and/or take on a lumpish viscosity, similar to gelatin desserts. However, if there is too much water in the broth for the amount of bones being used, then even good gelatin content may not be overtly apparent.

HCL, GERD AND GELATIN

Gelatin has a capacity to help us get more from the foods we eat, in turn helping us to heal tissues throughout our body. We really aren't what we eat—there is one more crucial step. We are actually what we digest and make useable in our body. And when we can put to use the wonderful, life-enhancing foods we are consuming, we make healthier, stronger new cells for healthier, stronger bodies. Consuming foods rich in gelatin from naturally-occurring sources, such as broth and stocks is a foundational way to heal the body.

Research has shown gelatin to actually benefit scenarios where people are producing too little hydrochloric acid (HCl) in their stomachs. Among its many functions, HCl is notably necessary for mineral breakdown, protection from pathogens, and the digestion of proteins. If a person is generating too little HCl, they will have difficulty with these processes...hence, potential mineral deficiencies. They are also open to more infections, such as H. pylori, implicated in many stomach ulcer diagnoses, and E. coli (interestingly, H. pylori is suspected to actually suppress HCl production, thus creating a more hospitable environment for it to thrive.), Low HCl also impedes the ability to break down proteins properly.

And of all the macronutrients—carbohydrates, fats and proteins—it could be argued that protein is the most integral to our body's composition and function. It is what makes our muscle fibers, the immunoglobulins of our immune system, the structure of our skeleton and various cellular metabolic processes, to name a few. Hence, a deficiency in HCl can be gravely detrimental to a person's wellbeing.

Interestingly, underproduction of HCl is often the root cause of a very common digestive disturbance—heartburn and gastroesophageal reflux disease (GERD.) In a nutshell, it works like this:

The autonomic nervous system responds to an increase in stomach acid when we eat by closing the sphincter that blocks the flow of stomach acid back up into the esophagus. If the production of HCl is too low, this mechanism is impaired, thus allowing the highly acid HCl to flow back into the esophagus. This leads to burning and tissue inflammation, because this stomach acid—even a small amount of it—is damaging to the unprotected tissues of the esophagus.

In response to such discomfort, people will often look to medications that *further* dampen the HCl, either directly (antacids such as TUMS, Alka-Seltzer and Rolaids) or through a physiological decrease in HCl production (Tagamet, Zantac and Prilosec, which block the production of HCl.) Regular use of such products can deepen issues related to low HCl availability in the upper GI tract.

So, when we see a simple food such as the naturally occurring gelatin in bone broth, benefiting our body's ability to use and produce HCl, it seems reasonable to include it regularly in our diets. In fact, when consuming gelatin with a meal, digestive action is spread evenly throughout the mass of food, and all components proceed more smoothly down the digestive tract. A cup of broth with a meal, or a couple ladle's worth used in the preparation of legumes or soaked grains, can be an excellent hedge against improper digestion of proteins and minerals.

HOW WE USE BONE BROTHS

Truth be known, although my training in Traditional Chinese Medicine demonstrated the functionality of a bone broth, it wasn't until recent-times that I made a point to keep one going rather constantly in our kitchen. Helping my sister to recover from the birth of her two children really got my interest spurred in the beneficial effect of broths for recovery. Studying more about their use in traditional foods as presented by author, food historian and researcher Sally Fallon Morrell and the Weston A. Price Foundation, pushed my interest further.

However, it was a routine dentist's visit that cinched the deal for me. **To my surprise, the dentist met me in the lobby to inform me that two of my son's primary teeth would need to be extracted due to cavities and abscesses.** From my hours of study in the matter, I believe this sort of scenario often develops when there is decreased mineralization, often due to a diet that leaches minerals or is poor in mineral content to begin with. Much of my son's diet as a youngster didn't involve the usual culprits of dental decay—processed sugars, chewy sweets, sodas—instead, he ate a lot of whole grains and, later, gluten-free grain products...all un-soaked, and in their commercially-prepared form.

The main issue with this as relates to mineralization is the anti-nutrients found in the un-soaked, unfermented grains—notably, *phytic acid*. Phytic acid has a strong ability to block the absorption of minerals, and humans do not generate the enzyme, phytase, that is needed to break down this common component of grains, legumes, nuts and seeds. Hence, a diet heavy in phytic acid-rich foods can have a significant impact on a person's mineral balance and reserves...and I believe my son's predilection for gluten-free toast, pizza, cereals, frozen waffles, etc.—all from organic sources, but definitely not soaked nor fermented before preparation—was key to his body's need to allocate its mineral reserves, leaving his teeth weakened enough to succumb to the bacteria in his mouth.

Once I saw the effects of what I'd thought had been more balanced dietary choices, I made some quick changes in our family's diet...notably, soaking and fermenting any grains before ingestion, and the regular consumption of bone broth.

These days, we keep a bone broth going regularly in our home. Rarely does our crockpot take a break! I may serve us each a cup in the morning with our breakfast of yogurt, fruit, eggs and homemade, toasted sourdough bread and butter. It is a rich and warming substitute for what had been a daily cup of organic coffee—and, rather than leaving me jittery, with blood sugar spikes and a demand on my mineral reserves, the broth delivers on balanced energy, better protein and mineral assimilation and level blood sugar. We stay full until lunch, with no need for snacks in between.

I'll use it to cook soaked grains at dinnertime, or as a hot liquid in the steaming of braised vegetables. Of course, it's a delight as a base for gravy, or for a quick soup of vegetables and meat, or with a cracked egg swirled in.

If we've really been on the go, then sometimes I'll add a portion of pastured liver or heart to the bones, thus creating a richer broth. The fatty acids, cell-nourishing cholesterols and fat-soluble vitamins that are replete in organs make their way into the broth as well.

Our rhythm of using the broth is as follows (though there are certainly other approaches):

- *Any meat that was on the bones in the broth, or was added at the beginning of the cooking process, we consume within the first day.*

- *Dependent on the size of bones (chicken, turkey and fish bones are smaller and break down much more quickly than the larger animals' bones), we may leave them for a second day.*

- *By the third day, we are finishing the broth, and beginning anew with fresh bones. If we've been using larger bones, I may add them back in to the new bones of a fresh broth. Doing so allows for different mineral composition breaking down into the broth.*

HOW TO MAKE YOUR OWN BONE BROTH

You'll see in the information to follow that I'm going to create these recipe suggestions around one of my most treasured kitchen tools—the crockpot. If you don't currently own one, or if yours is an older version, with only High and Low settings,

I encourage you to spend the $40 to $100 on a newer version. New models are generally oval in shape, making for a much more functional space for entire chickens, or larger bones, than the traditional circle shape.

However, a crockpot is not necessary. You can also use a stockpot on the stove, set on a low heat, which will follow a robust simmering period.

This method has its drawbacks—notably, maintaining the heat at the right temperature to keep pathogens at bay, but not so hot that the broth scorches on the bottom. And if working with a gas stove, the constant need for a low flame has its own dangers, not the least of which is a larger fire, as well as a gas leak should the flame be extinguished from drafts. That being said, stoves and hearths have been the traditional places to keep a broth going. This is just one instance when I really appreciate living in the 21st Century!

With an older crockpot, the High setting may be too hot, and the Low setting may be too cool. A rule of thumb is to keep the temperature at 180°F/82°C or above, for the longstanding heat required for these recipes. You can use a meat thermometer to gauge this. If the Low setting is less than this temperature, then you'll need to keep the pot set on High, but this may be considerably hotter than necessary, and can damage the proteins and other components of the broth, when kept at this temperature for the longer duration needed for these recipes. And if too low, then there is the very real concern for pathogenic activity.

So, my suggestion is to purchase a new crockpot, in the 5-6 quart size range, and with various temperature settings, either as a dial, or as pertains to cooking time. *And if you're starting with raw bones, joints and meats, be sure to start in the higher temperature range—say a 4-6 hour setting, or the highest temperature setting. After this period, the pot will shift into the Keep Warm setting*, where it will stay for the duration, if the directions are followed below (notably, the infusion of boiling water any time some of the broth has been drawn down—this keeps the potential from pathogenic trouble diminished, because the temperature will not be decreasing to the point allowable for pathogenic activity to flourish.)

There are many ways to start a broth. I'm going to outline a few, dependent on your frequency of use of the broth, and what you have to use as your base. As mentioned, **all of these recipes are using a 5-6 quart crockpot.**

METHOD 1 – NEW TO MAKING AND USING BROTHS? START HERE

If you are totally new to the concept of making a broth—as most are—then consider becoming comfortable using your crockpot by making bone-in, skin-on chicken pieces, from which a rich broth will be created. This is a terrific dish to prepare following breakfast for a world-class dinner that night. And the 10-15 minutes you're going to set aside to do so will be faster and incredibly healthier than the time it would take later that afternoon to stop in a fast food restaurant or purchase a rotisserie chicken from the grocery store!

CHICKEN SWIMMING IN ITS JUICES

SERVES 4-6
- *One whole, organic Chicken, cut into pieces, or a mix of 2-3 chicken thighs, a chicken breast, and 2-3 drumsticks—all meat cuts will be bone-in and skin-on*
- *2-3 tablespoons fresh Herbs* (or 1-2 teaspoons dried herbs), such as sage, tarragon or rosemary*
- *1-2 teaspoons Sea Salt, or to taste after cooking*
- *A small, finely-chopped Yellow Onion*
- *A clove of minced Garlic*
- *2 cups filtered Water, or 1 cup water and 1 cup organic White Wine*
- *The juice of a fresh Lemon (about 2-4 tablespoons)*

METHOD
Place all ingredients into a cool crockpot. Put the lid on, set to the 6-hour setting and walk away. If unopened, crockpots will maintain the liquid formed from the cooking process, and after this period, you'll notice that you have a lot of liquid remaining from your very tender and delectable chicken.

Remove the chicken from the pot and separate out the meat from the bones, setting the bones on a clean plate. Enjoy the meat immediately, or store it in a glass or ceramic container in the refrigerator for salads and sandwiches over the next few days. Drizzle the meat with some of the liquid from the crockpot. Place the bones that have been separated from the meat back in the remaining liquid in the crockpot. Add 4 or 5 cups of boiling water, a teaspoon or so of sea salt, a tablespoon of apple cider vinegar, and set on an 8-hour setting. (If you've been following the directions on when to do these steps, then you'll have your bone broth simmering through the night as you sleep.)

At the end of this period, the crockpot will shift to the Keep Warm setting and you'll have a delicious broth that you can enjoy as is, or to use as a base for soup, or to cook soaked grains or legumes. To store the broth in the refrigerator, simply ladle into glass, stainless steel or ceramic jars, straining it through a stainless steel sieve as it pours in. Plan to use the broth within four days if refrigerated. Once cooled in the refrigerator, you can then transfer it to freezer-safe containers, or even ice cube trays, to store for up to two months in the freezer.

This is a great primer for getting used to using your crockpot for meals, and then using what we would normally throw away—the bones—as the base for more broth.

Method 2 – For the Intermediate or Daily Consumer of Broth

Here's another method, starting with raw bones and other parts. This recipe is a good choice if you're not planning to eat a lot of the broth daily, instead consuming in the 1-4 cup a day range. This will allow you to get the terrific nutrition of a broth, but without the concern of it becoming scorched due to too much of it staying in a warm pot, where proteins can denature and fats can degrade:

Method
- Plan to start your broth with 2-3 Marrow, Feet, Neck or Shank Bones and a piece of Organ Meat if you like
- If you're using Chicken or Turkey, choose either whole birds, or cuts such as thighs, backs, drumsticks and necks that have the skin and bones intact; include the

giblets if they're available
- For Fish, include the entire head and all the bones

Add to this:
- 3-4 quarts filtered Water
- 2-4 tablespoons Celtic or Himalayan Sea Salt (best to start low and adjust flavor as needed after cooking)
- 2 tablespoons of Vinegar (usually raw apple cider vinegar, though others, such as organic balsamic vinegar or naturally fermented, unseasoned rice vinegar would work as well, dependent on the meats you're using.) You can also omit the vinegar and add an additional 2-3 tablespoons of fresh Lemon Juice
- Maybe some Wine — 1/2 cup or so, preferably organic
- A chopped Onion
- You might also add a little bit of Seaweed — a couple of pieces of *dulse* or *kombu*, a small sheet of *nori*, 1-2 pieces of *wakame* — any of these choices is fine. Doing so will increase the iodine composition of the broth, an important nutrient missing from the diets of those who don't consume a lot of seafood and who use natural sea salts that are not commercially-iodized. (Personally, I like the flavor of the dulse the best.)

Place everything into a cool crockpot, and set it on the 4-hour setting. Fill the pot with enough water to leave only about 1.5″ of space at the top, and cover with the lid. Walk away. At the end of the 4-hour setting, it will kick into the Keep Warm setting. If your crockpot does not have an automatic Keep Warm temperature shift, then manually turn it to the Low setting and keep an eye on the temperature to insure it's at least at 180° F/82° C, simmering gently.

Using this method you'll likely have a broth that is incredibly rich–sometimes so rich, a splash of vinegar or lemon or lime juice in each serving is helpful to cut the oiliness of this first draft, or you might allow each cup of drawn broth to cool and skim some of the fat off to use later to sauté vegetables. This first draft is also excellent for cooking soaked grains or potatoes — it will infuse these foods with the richest, most savory flavor. If you do separate some fat out, just be sure to use it — it's full of cell-healing cholesterol and saturated fats!

Using a stainless steel sieve, strain off the solids from the liquid, and store the broth for up to four days in glass, ceramic or steel containers in the refrigerator, or use immediately. Separate out the bones from the skin, organs, fat and meat. Use the edible portions in other dishes—they are incredibly tender after a long, warm cooking.

From your separated bones you can make a fresh batch of broth. After the long first cooking, you may find that the bones are beginning to crush easily.

For reusing your bones:

• Add to them 3-5 quarts of fresh Water

• An additional 2 tablespoons of Vinegar or fresh Lemon Juice

• 1-3 tablespoons of Celtic Sea Salt

If you can, break the bones open (as with smaller chicken and turkey bones) so the marrow can infuse into the broth. Set on the 8-hour setting, allowing more of the bones' mineral composition to break down into solution. As before, the pot will either shift to the Keep Warm setting on its own, or you'll need to set it on the Low setting manually.

This broth will taste different than the first—it likely won't be as strong nor as oily. Feel free to add vegetables, seasonings and meat toward the last couple of hours of cooking, to enrich both flavor and nutrition (just be sure to remove the bones before you eat it!) **Or, you can skip the additional ingredients, and simply combine this second batch of broth to the remainder of the first batch of broth, and store the combination of the two in the refrigerator to consume over the next couple of days.**

This method of straining off the broth from the solids at the end of each cooking period is a good choice when you're not using too much of the broth at a time—broth left on the Keep Warm setting on the pot will take on a burned flavor, which, in my mind, means that there are unhealthy degradations of fat and protein. Better to keep it fresh!

METHOD 3 – FOR THE ADVANCED CONSUMER OF BROTH, EATING A LOT DAILY

If you intend to use a good portion of your broth each day, then consider this method. This option is also good for a 3-4 day broth fast.

METHOD

You'll start everything as you did Method 2—same ingredients, same cooking times. However, after your 24-hour cycle, plan to consume at least half (if not more) of your broth each day. Also remove any meaty bits after the first day, to enjoy either as a soup in a bowl of the broth, or in some other dish.

Since you're going to be adding so much fresh, hot water to the pot to bring it back up to its original level, you will be removing many of the fats and proteins that otherwise would have overcooked in this continual process.

For each successive day:

- Bring the level of liquid back up to the original amount with fresh, hot Water *every time* you remove some of the broth to consume

- Add Celtic Sea Salt to taste, usually a pinch to a teaspoon is sufficient

- Add 1 teaspoon Vinegar, or a tablespoon of Lemon or Lime juice if you like, to continue to demineralize the bone

- Add a sprinkle of Seaweed, too, from time-to-time, to keep the iodine and other trace minerals up in the broth

- Keep the crockpot on the Keep Warm setting

- On about the third day, and sixth day, add another meaty bone to the mix to bring up the fat and amino acid content. Bring the heat back up to the High/6-Hour setting, then allow it to drop to the Keep Warm setting. Strain off and consume the meat and other soft tissue portions within 24 hours.

Use this method for up to a week. If your broth starts to taste burned or old, you are moving through it too slowly, and may want to use the Method 2 instead. Also, make sure that your Keep Warm/Low setting isn't boiling. The activity should be just a very low simmer. Anything higher, for an extended period of time, will damage proteins and fats.

METHOD 4 – FOR THE ON-THE-GO USER

Finally, if you're intending to do a "short-run" of the broth, to be completed in total over 3 days (a good option if you're visiting somewhere for the weekend, or if you just have a short window of time for cooking), this is a good option.

METHOD
Begin in the same manner, with the same ingredients and cooking times as listed for Method 2, but then do as follows:

By the end of the first 24-hour period, plan to remove all the soft tissues (organs, meat, skin.) Use them in other dishes—after such a long, slow cooking, they are very tender. If you're working with smaller bones from poultry or fish, remove these on the first day with the soft tissues.

If you're using bigger bones, you can keep these in the broth for another day, on the Keep Warm setting. Add back to the broth enough boiling water to bring it to the original level, a teaspoon or so of sea salt, a tablespoon of lemon juice or vinegar, and cover.

By the end of the second day, remove the bones, and finish your broth, which can be kept at the Keep Warm setting for another day, if you like, or poured into a glass, ceramic or stainless steel carafe and stored in the refrigerator. Reheat on the stovetop as needed, and consume within three days. (If you need to store it longer, place the refrigerated broth into freezer-safe containers and store for future use for up to two months in the freezer.)

DIRECTIONS FOR MAKING BROTH WITH BONES THAT ARE ALREADY COOKED

As mentioned, another option is to start with the bones from a roasted chicken or turkey, or the ribs or other bones from a long, slow cooking of beef or lamb, where the meat literally falls from the bones, allowing you to separate out the bones before they've made it to the table.

METHOD

If you use bones that have already been cooked, place them in the crockpot with all the other recommended ingredients and proportions (onion, water, vinegar/lemon juice, salt, wine if you like) from Methods 2-4, but instead select the 8-hour cooking time (or, if using a pot with only High and Low settings, begin on the High setting for an hour or two to soften the onion, then set to Low.) From this start, you can move through any of the Methods listed above that best fit your needs.

CONSIDERATIONS

• Do be certain to add back in the same amount of boiling water that you withdraw from the broth if you are using the same bones for two or three days—it really is important that the proteins and fats in the broth don't degrade from getting too hot in a concentrated bit of liquid. Adding fresh, hot water can help to keep this from happening. Taste and season accordingly once water has been added.

• If the broth is too oily for your palate, place the cup in the refrigerator for 20 minutes. This will allow the fat to rise to the top and form an easily-removed disc of saturated fat that can be saved in a glass bowl for cooking other foods over the next few days.

• Make certain that your Keep Warm/Low setting does not boil. The temperature should allow for the gentlest of simmering, or just below the simmer. Anything higher than this for long periods will degraded fats and proteins.

- If you want additional seasonings, vegetables or herbs included in your broth, *add them after the initial long cooking if you're reusing your bones*. Spices, vegetables and herbs can take on unpalatable flavors if cooked for two or three days. I add additional ingredients when I am ready to use the broth as a base for another dish: Soup, stews, beans, grains, etc. (*Note, this rule doesn't apply to Method 1—that is a shorter cooking time from the beginning, and you'll be simply adding already-cooked bones to fresh water for the second cooking.)

Making a broth is something that might be very new to many of us, but with a little practical application, you'll soon be wondering how you ever lived without it! Its flavor and nutrition make it an indispensable component to a well-rounded, traditional food kitchen.

The tools and products of making water kefir

MAKING WATER KEFIR

The simple ingredients and tools for making water kefir

Water kefir is an easy to make, inexpensive and versatile lacto-fermented beverage. It is mildly effervescent, just slightly sweet and lends itself to being a refreshing and nutritious base to other ingredients. It's also a terrific starter to other lacto-ferments, such as soaked and fermented grains and cultured vegetables. As with all fermented foods, there will be a very small amount of alcohol generated (usually far less than 1%.) Just keep this in mind if alcohol consumption at any level is a concern.

A Little on the History of Water Kefir

Also called *tibicos*, Japanese water crystals, sugar kefir grain and California bees, water kefir is the by-product of a symbiotic community of bacteria and yeast (known as a *SCOBY*) transforming sugared water into a fermented, gently effervescent drink.

It is a type of beverage that is used the world over, with slight variations in the composition of the SCOBY, based on the conditions of the region in which it's being used (these variations are actually seen kitchen-to-kitchen, as the SCOBY is influenced by the various microscopic inhabitants of each home.) Tibicos is thought to derive from the Mexican *Opuntia* cactus (commonly known as *nopales*), on the pads of which form hard granules that can be reconstituted in a sugar-water medium.

Dehydrated kefir grains

From left to right, strained water kefir grains, freshly-made sugar water with kefir grains on the bottom and water kefir that has been strained and is ready to enjoy.

WHY YOU SHOULD MAKE YOUR OWN WATER KEFIR

Water kefir is rich in many of the B Vitamins, Vitamin K, digestion-supporting enzymes and beneficial bacteria and yeasts. The kefir grains consume the dissolved sugar solids, generating lactic acid, ethanol, carbon dioxide (CO_2.)

Many are familiar with milk kefir, another probiotic-rich, mildly effervescent cultured beverage. It too is the end product of a SCOBY transformation. The difference, however, is that its culturing medium is the lactose (milk sugar) in milk, rather than the sugar water; there are differences, as well, in the composition of the SCOBY itself.

With water kefir, there is very little chance for allergic reaction as there can be with many other fermented beverages that are dairy-based, such as milk kefir and yogurt. And because it does not rely on caffeine as is needed in another popular cultured drink, *kombucha*, it is a useable beverage for those wishing to abstain from caffeine. All that is required is de-chlorinated and filtered water, sugar, the water kefir SCOBY (generally referred to as water kefir grains) and possibly a little mineral supplement if one is working with reverse osmosis or distilled water (mineral-rich spring water is the best choice.)

The appearance of the water kefir grains definitely begs the question, "What is in there?" As mentioned, there are numerous beneficial bacteria and yeasts. Generally speaking, water kefir grains are comprised of *Streptococcus, Lactobacillus, Leuconostoc* and *Pediococcus* bacteria, and yeast strains of *Kloeckera, Candida and Saccharomyces*; it is the *Lactobacillus brevis* that has been identified as the source for the polymer structure that looks quite similar to translucent oat groats.

And while there are commercially-available water kefir beverages, the cost-savings and ease of creation make producing your own water kefir at home a simple and nutritious option.

On the left, rehydrated water kefir grains; on the right, dehydrated milk kefir grains, a typical format in which the SCOBY can be shipped and stored.

HOW WE USE WATER KEFIR

We make a fresh batch of water kefir at least every couple of days and never run out of ideas on how to use it! Of course, it is a refreshing base for other beverages (see *Flavoring Ideas for Water Kefir*), or sipped without any adornment. A quarter cup is a terrific quaff just before a meal, to help stimulate digestion. We also use it to ferment soaked grains, from sprouted brown rice to oatmeal to breads (see *How to Properly Soak Grains*.) It is an excellent starter to other ferments (see *Fermented Vegetables*), priming the fermentation activity with loads of beneficial bacteria.

HOW TO MAKE WATER KEFIR

If starting with dehydrated water kefir grains, you'll need to first rehydrate them to bring them to an active state. Many companies ship the grains dehydrated, allowing the end user to make them when ready, and for the portability and durability of dehydrated grains in transport. If your grains come to you dehydrated, keep them in the refrigerator until you're ready to put them to use. (See *Resources* section for water kefir grain sources.)

Once ready, place them in sweetened room temperature water. This ratio will be about 4 cups filtered, de-chlorinated water to 5 or 6 tablespoons sugar (you will likely need to heat the water to allow the sugar crystals to melt into solution—simply allow it to cool to room temperature before adding the kefir grains.) Leave the grains in the sweetened water at room temperature for 3-4 days, and no longer than 5. During this time, they may generate water kefir that is mildly carbonated and considerably less sweet than the original, sweetened water. Once rehydrated, you're ready to use them on a regular basis!

WHAT YOU WILL NEED

- De-chlorinated, filtered water (if using distilled or reverse osmosis water, you might need a few drops of liquid minerals such as ConcenTrace Trace Minerals, or a quarter teaspoon baking soda, or a quarter teaspoon of Himalayan or Celtic Sea Salt)—Filtered spring water is best
- Sugar, preferably organic (if using a mineral-rich sugar, such as Raw Coconut Crystals

or Rapadura—something with a lot of inherent color due to its mineral content being intact—you may not need the additional minerals for distilled or reverse osmosis water)
- Rehydrated Water Kefir grains
- Glass quart jar with a screw-top lid (it is best to avoid metals and plastics as they can react with the acids in the water kefir)
- Fine mesh strainer, preferably plastic or some other non-metal

Water kefir, strained of grains and ready to enjoy

8 EASY STEPS

- In a quart jar, dissolve 4-5 tablespoons' sugar into ¼ cup hot water and stir well to bring the sugar into solution.
- Next, add enough cool water to bring the liquid total to an inch or so shy of the brim.
- Allow the water to cool to room temperature and add the kefir grains.
- Cover the jar with the lid. This will keep dust and any insects out of the water and will

allow for some carbonation to build.

- Leave the mixture at room temperature (65°–78°F /18°-26°C) for 24 to 48 hours. Do not allow the water kefir to sit longer than 72 hours, as the grains can begin to starve from a lack of sugar in the solution. At this point, the kefir can start to taste much more like vinegar, as the acetic acids take over.
- At its completion, you will likely notice little bubbles that rise to the top if the jar is tilted. You may notice a difference in the color—if you used a mineral-rich, brownish sugar, the finished product may be lighter (see photo.) If you used a white sugar, the finished liquid should be more opaque. And the taste should be significantly less sweet than the beginning sugar solution, as the sugar should have been consumed in great quantity by the kefir grains. It may or may not be mildly carbonated.
- Strain the kefir grains from the liquid. Simply pour the water kefir through a small plastic or bamboo strainer into another glass jar. Cover the strained water kefir jar with a tight-fitting lid and store either in the refrigerator or on the counter—it does not require refrigeration, though if left at room temperature for a few days it will become much more acidic.
- Begin with your reserved kefir grains to make a new batch, starting at Step 1.

SOME CONSIDERATIONS

- You may notice quite a change in appearance of the finished water kefir from the sugar water it had been a day or 2 prior. It may be lighter in color if you're using a mineral-rich sugar, or it may become opaque if you've used a lighter, less mineral-rich sugar. Both of these outcomes are normal. The flavor should be less sweet, and there should be a very mild scent of a cultured food—not quite tart, but lively in the nose.

- If your water kefir ferments for too long, or the temperature is too warm, the acetic acids may take over, making for a vinegar-like flavor. While this may not be so palatable for drinking, it is fine to consume. Use it in place of regular vinegar in a salad dressing. Also, fi the temperature is too warm, day after day, the water kefir can take on strong, "off" flavors. If your temperature is too warm, place your water kefir in the refrigerator after making it, and allow about a day for the fermentation to occur.

- It is best to avoid using honey as a sweetener for the sugar water. While it might impart a wonderful flavor, its antibacterial nature can, over time, damage the water kefir grains. Better to stick with other sugars. Additionally, sugar alcohols like Xylitol, and non-sugary natural "sweeteners" like stevia and *lo han guo* will not work as a fuel source for the water kefir grains, as they do not contain the needed carbohydrates in the sugars.

- If you are going on vacation or need to take a break from making your water kefir, place the kefir grains in a glass jar, in which about 1 cup of water and 2 tablespoons of sugar have been dissolved (this is assuming you have about 2 tablespoons or less of grains. If it's more than this, use a proportionately greater amount of water and sugar.) Cover and place in the refrigerator for up to 2 weeks. If you'll be gone longer than this, try to find a friend to feed the grains new sugar water at least every 2 weeks, and keep the combination stored in the refrigerator. While the fermentation process is greatly slowed, it is not halted by refrigeration. You can also try low-heat dehydration of your kefir grains. Place them on a piece of parchment paper in the dehydrator and set no higher than 105°/41°C and dehydrate until completely dry. Store in the refrigerator until ready to rehydrate.

Adding kefir grains to fresh, sweetened water to begin the process again

FLAVORING IDEAS FOR WATER KEFIR

Water kefir flavored with fresh ginger

It is easy and fun to flavor water kefir. Our family enjoys it "straight up," but it is also a terrific base for homemade, nutritious beverages. Consider the water kefir a sort of blank slate to your imagination. It's mild effervescence is a delightful backdrop to most fruity and sweet flavors.

SOME IDEAS TO ADD TO A QUART OF PREPARED WATER KEFIR (FROM WHICH THE WATER KEFIR GRAINS HAVE BEEN REMOVED)

- Add ½ cup of freshly made organic apple juice (or even store-bought), tightly cap, and leave at room temperature for 12-24 hours to produce a carbonated, lightly-sweet drink. Just be careful about excessive carbonation—check the bottle occasionally to release pressure and avoid the risk of spilling over or even explosion (this is very rare, and releasing pressure during the fermentation process will alleviate this concern.) The additional sugar in the juice may slightly increase the alcohol content of the finished beverage, so be mindful of this if serving to children or someone for whom alcohol is a concern.

- Blend 1cup fresh or frozen organic pineapple chunks with ½ cup coconut water and add to the water kefir. Serve immediately, or cap and allow to ferment a few hours longer before serving.

- Blend 1 cup of fresh or frozen organic blueberries (or raspberries, strawberries, pomegranate seeds or any combination of all) with a ½ teaspoon of organic orange or lemon zest and a tablespoon or two of raw honey. Add the water kefir and a cup of ice, blend again until slushy and serve immediately.

- Use any of the all-natural flavored stevia liquids…a few drops of citrus, berry and/or vanilla-based flavors, would be a delicious, healthy, sugar-free option in lieu of diet sodas or other diet drinks. Likewise, using organic, all-natural flavor extracts such as orange or lemon, combined with a little stevia and vanilla extract, is another sugar-free, all-natural way to enhance the flavor of water kefir.

- Adding ¼ to ½ cup of freshly-made lemon or lime juice (to your tartness preference), a scant ½ teaspoon Celtic or Himalayan Sea Salt and 4-5 tablespoons of raw honey, yacon syrup or grade B maple syrup will result in a delicious take on lemonade or limeade (I like to add a sprinkle of cayenne pepper on top—delicious!) You could also add a pinch of freshly-ground ginger. Excellent in the summer months!

FLAVORING THE WATER KEFIR WHILE IT'S FERMENTING

- Another option is to flavor the water kefir during fermentation. To do this, simply take a few slices of organic lemon, lime, orange or grapefruit rind and stir them into the mixture as you begin a fresh batch of water kefir. 3 or 4 quarter-sized slices of organic ginger would be a great choice, too. At the end of the fermentation, simply remove the rind or ginger before serving.

HOMEMADE YOGURT

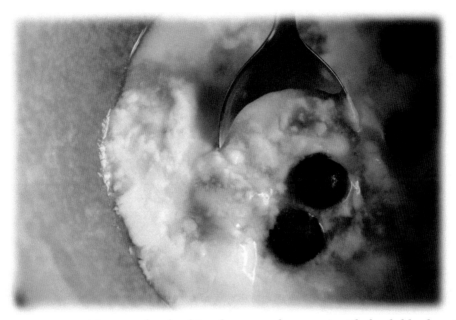

Delicious, tart, nutritious and refreshing homemade yogurt with fresh blueberries and vanilla

Culturing dairy milk is one of those traditional food techniques that I'm certain someone simply witnessed when fresh milk was left too long in the bucket on a warm day. The enzymes and inherent bacteria in raw milk lend themselves toward fermentation—that is why raw milk sours rather than spoils like pasteurized milk. However, it was the harnessing of the right conditions, the right bacteria, and perpetuating everything for the right amount of time, that has become the tradition of various dairy culturing, from Parmesan cheese to milk kefir to yogurt.

SOME HISTORY ON YOGURT

As with many of the old food preparation techniques, no one is quite certain how yogurt developed into being a widely propagated and consumed food. However, it is generally held that as a perpetual and intentional practice (rather than the naturally-occurring, random ferment) it is at least 6000 years old. It likely came about during the time of animal domestication, when Neolithic man in central Asia began consuming the milk of kept animals. In order to transport and contain this milk, the stomachs of animals were likely used; these vessels would have contained residual acids and bacteria that would lend themselves to the coagulation of the milk proteins. With the right warm temperatures, the milk would sour in these unique conditions, the resultant food being pleasantly tart with a thicker texture than the milk that was placed in the vessels. Additionally, it was likely soon recognized that this sour, thick milk kept much longer than milk simply placed in earthen pots.

The word yogurt is derived from the Turkish word meaning "to curdle or to thicken." A staple food through much of the Middle East for thousands of years, it has also been part of the Eastern European diet for hundreds of years. But it was in the early 1900's when Isaac Carasso, a Spanish doctor, made yogurt into a commercial product. Having used yogurt to treat patients suffering from digestive diseases, he founded *Groupe Danone* after perfecting the first industrial process for making yogurt. Today, we know this company as Dannon.

WHY SHOULD WE CULTURE DAIRY PRODUCTS?

Culturing dairy reduces the lactose (milk sugar) in the milk, transforming it into a rich source of immune-building beneficial bacteria* that is lower in naturally-occurring sugars and higher in Vitamins B and C.

How often have we been told to eat yogurt after a round of antibiotics? This practice is not only folk medicine; research supports the gut- and immunity-benefits of yogurt consumption. From cancer to digestive ills to asthma, the role of yogurt as a therapeutic agent has been shown again and again.

Culturing dairy generally makes it much more digestible by breaking down the casein (milk protein) into easier to digest amino acids and peptides. Lactic acid bacteria—the beneficial microbes that turn milk into yogurt, cheese and other dairy ferments—generate enzymes that have protein-breaking qualities. Casein is a protein in milk that can be very problematic for many to digest, but with the right bacteria working on the milk, it can be transformed and better tolerated by many.

Culturing dairy increases the enzymes in the milk* (even pasteurized milk that is then cultured has a boost to its enzyme capacity), which helps to digest the components of the milk and lightens the load on the body's digestive enzymes. As mentioned, enzymatic activity is unleashed by the lacto-bacteria's consumption of milk sugars. In the wake of this activity, countless enzymes are generated that help to lighten the enzyme load our saliva, pancreas and liver must create to digest our food. With enzyme-rich food, we are giving our systems a break!

(*For both enzymes and bacteria to be present, the yogurt cannot be heated above 105°F/40.5°C after the milk is cultured. Heat destroys enzymes at 105°F/40.5°C, and most cultures around 115°F/46°C.)

How We Use Yogurt in Our Kitchen

Making yogurt was our original, homegrown foray into eating more traditionally prepared foods. As I look back on it, I find it interesting that this was where it all started, as soaking grains and nuts would have likely been simpler, even making broth might have been an easier choice. But there was something about the blatant alchemy of milk becoming yogurt, and this process happening to this day in many kitchens across Europe and Asia (and a few in North America!), that spoke to me.

So, with some goat's milk and *Yogourmet* cultures from the natural foods' section of our local grocery store, I began making yogurt. And like all of these traditions that we've brought into the flow of our lives, this one has had its own learning curve.

These are some items I want to share from the start, things I've learned through trial, error, and trying again:

• I've learned that if the culturing temperature is too warm for too long, everything separates out, with curds and watery whey as my end product. Eventually, this will also take on the scent of acetone—not so appealing.

- I've learned that if I don't let the milk culture long enough, or if the temperature is too cool, the top of the yogurt will appear cultured, but when poured into a bowl, uncultured milk beneath this set top layer will come pouring forth—no through-and-through culturing has happened.

- I've learned that if one chooses to use the "Backslopping" method below, there is a critical mass that happens when simply reusing the same jar by topping off with freshly prepared milk. This was a time saving measure I used for one less jar to wash. Too much of "time-saving," though, and even the strongest of yogurt cultures will fall to mold spores. Best to always transfer yesterday's yogurt starter to a new jar, add the prepared milk and start fresh.

- And, once we started using raw milk, I long resisted the step of making a "mother batch," which keeps the inherent cultures in the raw milk from competing with the yogurt cultures. And because of this resistance, I've learned that what should be a re-useable culture will actually have a rather short life. After a fashion, each new batch will be more watery than the last, eventually petering out all together. So, now we make a mother batch once a week—it is just worth the little extra effort.

Heating raw milk to make a mother batch of yogurt for the week

Even with the forgiving, artisanal nature of traditional food preparation, there are reasons why there are some set rules, and it's just a good idea to follow them. Please keep my attempts to cut a few corners in mind as you set out to make your own yogurt!

What is left of last night's yogurt, after this morning's breakfast

MAKING YOGURT AT HOME

Milk with cultures, going into the yogurt maker

The easiest way to make yogurt is to purchase a yogurt maker, which is essentially an incubator that keeps the temperature at a stable 110°F/43°C, the temperature at which most *thermophilic* (heat-loving) cultures thrive. This is not a mandatory tool, however. Here are other options:

- You can instead use a *mesophilic* culture, which cultures dairy in the 70°-78°F/21–25.5°C range. Purchase mesophilic cultures online (See the *References* section.)
- You can use a makeshift stable heat source, monitored with a food thermometer, to keep the culturing milk in the 110°F/43°C, and use thermophilic cultures.

Consider the following as makeshift incubating chambers:

- An insulated bag or ice chest, containing bottles filled with hot water—just keep the thermometer in the culturing milk, to make certain the temperature doesn't get too hot or cold.
- A food dehydrator with the trays removed, set at the 110° F/43°C setting.
- An oven or microwave warmed by its incandescent bulb, possibly with bottles of hot water inside to increase the heat if necessary. Again, just keep the thermometer in the cultured milk for monitoring.
- Set in the shade on a very warm summer's day (such as in the desert southwest). This can be a little tricky—use the thermometer to monitor closely.
- A tight-fitting insulator around a jar in which the milk has been brought to 110°F/43°C. Mylar bubble wrap, surrounded by a thick towel, would be a good option. Keep the thermometer in the milk to monitor.

In any of the above options, it's important to start with whole, organic milk, preferably from pastured animals, and raw if you can find it. (You can use skim or low-fat milk, but the end result will be less rich in flavor and thinner in consistency.) Pasteurized and vat pasteurized milk will work, but avoid using ultra-pasteurized milk. There are also pasteurized, non-homogenized whole milks at natural foods' stores.

You can use goat, sheep, buffalo, camel or cow milk; goat milk tends to make a thinner yogurt. If you use raw milk, you'll need to make a "mother batch" of starter yogurt (see directions below), otherwise the innate bacteria in the raw milk will eventually weaken and override the yogurt cultures.

You can also start homemade yogurt from a small, fresh, six-to-eight ounce container of organic, plain, live-culture, unsweetened yogurt. Look for one without additional thickeners or gums. You would then treat this as a thermophilic starter, adding a couple tablespoons of the container's contents to your quart of warmed milk (see important instructions below on sterilizing pasteurized milk), and keeping it in the thermophilic temperature range for culturing. This method will generally only produce one additional batch of yogurt, however (this is an example of a direct-set, or single use, culturing.)

If you're wishing to make yogurt from the same cultures again and again--a technique known as "back-slopping"--it is best to purchase cultures that are bred for this purpose (defined as reusable cultures.) This is the most cost-effective process, and the one that will be outlined below.

INSTRUCTIONS FOR MAKING YOGURT WITH THERMOPHILIC, REUSABLE CULTURES

For pasteurized milk
Using a thermometer, heat a quart of milk on the stovetop to 160°F/71°C. Keep the milk at this temperature for a few minutes to sterilize it.

This is an important step as pasteurized milk is devoid of naturally-occurring beneficial bacteria that can keep dangerous bacteria in check. Pasteurized milk thus becomes a medium that is rich in lactose (milk sugar), which makes it a potential breeding ground for dangerous bacteria. Bringing pasteurized milk only to the 110°F/43°C mark will create an environment that pathogenic bacteria would thrive in—warm and sweet. To avoid this possibility, heat it to 160°-180°F/71°-82°C, and then allow it to cool to about 110°F/43°C. Heating milk to this temperature has the added benefit of changing the structure of the milk proteins, making a thicker yogurt. Do check the temperature of the yogurt before adding the cultures—anything over 118°F/48°C will kill the yogurt cultures.

Gently bringing milk to a boil for sterilization

For raw milk

You can heat the milk to the 160°F/71°C range as was done for the pasteurized milk. While this will destroy any of the beneficial bacteria and enzymes in the raw milk, it will make for a firmer yogurt because of the change in protein structure, allowing for better coagulation. However, if you would like to maintain the native bacteria and enzymes in the raw milk, simply bring it to the 110°F/43°C range, either on the stovetop with a thermometer, or in the culturing jar in the incubating environment.

Once taken to the correct culturing temperature of 110°F/43°C, pour the milk into the quart-sized glass jar (unless you've been warming raw milk in it already in an incubation chamber), add your cultures and stir well to incorporate into the milk. *Before doing this, read the information on creating a mother batch below.*

Directions for Brand-new, Dehydrated Cultures

For sterilized, pasteurized milk

To make a quart of yogurt, place ½ teaspoon of dehydrated cultures into 2 cups of sterilized milk. Stir well, and pour in the remainder of the sterilized milk, bringing it to about an inch or 2 under the jar's brim. Cover with a cloth or paper towel, cinch with a rubber band and place in the yogurt maker or other incubation chamber. Check after 5 hours to see if yogurt has set; if not, keep checking every 30 minutes or so. (You'll know it's set, because it will all move as one unit away from the sides of the jar when tilted. It will also take on a lovely tart scent.) In bringing dormant cultures back to active function, it may take up to 12 hours—be patient, and do check them every half hour. Once set, place the jar on the counter at room temperature for a couple of hours, then enjoy or cover with a food-grade lid and refrigerate. *Be sure to reserve about a quarter cup of yogurt to start the next batch (backslopping), and use it within a week to avoid degradation of the yogurt cultures.*

For raw milk--creating a Mother Batch

It will be important to first create a mother batch of yogurt. This first, simple step allows for the reuse of yogurt cultures with the native bacteria in raw milk present. If raw milk is simply cultured without first sterilizing, over time the milk's innate bacteria will weaken the potency of the yogurt's bacteria, eventually leading to an inability to reuse the yogurt to start a new batch. Therefore, creating a small batch of sterilized milk, which will be the "mother" to cultures throughout the week, is important to maintain the integrity of the yogurt cultures. Once prepared, use most of this batch to start your raw milk yogurt for a week; reserve at least a tablespoon and use it as a starter to a new mother batch on day 7. Waiting any longer can significantly degrade the starter cultures. (If at the end of a week there is more than a tablespoon remaining of the mother batch, it can be consumed as regular yogurt.)

Using a thermometer, heat 1 cup of raw milk on the stovetop to at least 160°F/71°C, but no hotter than 180°F/82°C. Allow it to cool to around 110°F/43°C, then add 1/8 teaspoon of dehydrated starter culture and stir well to incorporate into the now sterilized milk. Transfer to a small glass jar, cover with a cloth cinched with a paper towel, and place in the yogurt maker or some other incubation chamber. Begin checking for coagulation and tartness around 4 hours. If the milk has not set, just check it again every half hour. In bringing dormant cultures back to active function, it may take up to 12 hours—be patient, and do check them every half hour. Once the milk has become yogurt, remove from the heat source and cool on the counter at room temperature for 2 hours. Cap tightly with a food-grade lid and place in the refrigerator. Plan to start a new mother batch, with a reserved tablespoon of the most-recent batch, within 7 days.

Making a small mother batch, to start many jars of yogurt through the week.

DIRECTIONS FOR REUSING YOGURT FROM A PREVIOUS BATCH OF PASTEURIZED MILK (BACKSLOPPING)

Using a thermometer, heat a quart of pasteurized milk on the stovetop and bring it to 160°-180°F/71°-82°C. Let the milk cool to 110°F/43°C, and pour it into a glass quart jar. (If you are interested in using any thickeners, incorporate them at this stage, stirring well—see *How to Flavor and Thicken Yogurt*.)

Add ¼ cup of yogurt from the previous batch, stir well into the sterilized milk and cover and cinch the jar with a paper towel. Place in the incubation chamber at 110°F/43°C and begin checking around 5 hours to see if it has set. If not, check back about every hour until it has become yogurt. Once complete, cool at room temperature for 2 hours before enjoying or storing in the refrigerator.

DIRECTIONS FOR MAKING RAW MILK YOGURT FROM THE MOTHER BATCH

To make a quart of raw milk yogurt, use a thermometer and bring your milk temperature to 110°F/43°C. (If you choose to heat the milk for a thicker consistency—but at the cost of loss of enzymes and inherent bacteria—then first heat to 160°F/71°C and cool to 110°F/43°C. Also, if you are planning to add any thickeners, incorporate them at this stage—see *Other Considerations* below.) Add 2 tablespoons of the mother batch of yogurt (do not use the yogurt from a previous batch as you would with backslopping sterilized milk yogurt), stir well to incorporate into the milk, cover and cinch with a paper towel, and place in incubation chamber for 5 hours; if the milk has not turned to yogurt by the 5-hour mark, keep checking on it every half hour or so. Once complete, place on the counter to cool at room temperature for a couple of hours, before consuming or capping with a food grade lid and refrigerating. *Plan to enjoy this entire quart of yogurt within a week—no need to reserve any amount as a starter to a new batch as you would with the backslopping technique. That is the role of the mother batch.*

The new mother batch, from which a couple of spoonsful of last week's mother batch has been added to the sterilized raw milk. This will go in the yogurt maker to be the new mother batch.

Raw milk going into a quart jar, to which a few spoonsful of the mother batch will be added

The mother batch being added to the milk

OTHER CONSIDERATIONS

- Since lactose is the food source for the yogurt cultures, do not use lactose-free milk when making yogurt (however, it is because of the consumption of the lactose by the bacteria that many lactose-sensitive individuals are able to enjoy yogurt without distress.)

- Whether making sterilized, pasteurized milk yogurt, or raw milk yogurt, plan to consume each batch within 5 days of production.

- Do not wait any longer than 7 days before making a new batch of yogurt, either from back-slopping sterilized, pasteurized milk yogurt, or from a mother batch of yogurt for raw milk. Significant degradation of the viable yogurt cultures will likely result if you wait any longer.

- If you wish to take a break from making yogurt, 7-9 days is the maximum to allow between making batches. If you'll be gone longer than this, but wish to maintain the viability of your cultures, you will need to have someone make a new batch of backslopped yogurt or a mother batch at least every 7 days. If this is not an option, then plan to just start over with new, dehydrated cultures when you are ready to resume production.

- If you wish to make less yogurt per batch than the quart amount suggested above, *simply use a ratio of 2 teaspoons of yogurt (either reserved or mother batch, dependent on your choice of milk) per 1 cup of milk.*

- The longer a yogurt is left to culture, the tarter and firmer it will become, as the bacteria consume more of the sweet lactose. Therefore, if you would like a yogurt with a stronger flavor, slightly firmer texture and less lactose, allow it culture longer. (Note that raw milk yogurt will always be thinner in consistency than milk heated to 160°F/71°C.)

  However, there will come a point where the yogurt will parse out to curds and whey (*see photo*.) Once this begins to happen, the bacteria will be without their needed lactose as a food source and will start dying off.

Yogurt that has cultured too long, or at too high a heat, becomes curds and whey.

The whey is a very nutritious source of bio-available minerals, enzymes, beneficial bacteria, amino acids and vitamins; strain and drink it, or use it as a base for a smoothie. If you do strain the whey off, it will keep up to six months in a clean, glass jar in the refrigerator (see *Uses for Whey*.) If you would rather not strain it, you can also just stir it into the curds (milk solids) and have a tart, slightly lumpy version of yogurt. This change in texture is a very small issue if the yogurt is blended into a smoothie, or used in a blended, prepared salad dressing.

Curds and whey can also develop if the culturing temperature was too fast, as can happen if the temperature is even a few degrees too warm. This is all-the-more reason to keep a thermometer on hand and begin checking for the yogurt's doneness at the 5-hour mark. For your first few batches, do keep a close eye on your temperature and times, to get an idea of the characteristics of your unique culturing environment.

If using a backslopping technique, you can stir the curds and whey together and attempt to use them to start a new batch. Watch times and temperatures very closely for the new batch; if a good, well-set batch is created, then the cultures remained viable. If not, then you may need to start over with a new set of dehydrated cultures. (This is not a concern if using a mother batch, as each batch's "doneness" will have no impact on each subsequent batch.)

Pasteurized Milk	Raw Milk
For the 1st Batch with Dehydrated Cultures	**For the 1st Batch with Dehydrated Cultures**
On the stovetop, heat 4 cups of milk to 160°F/71°C, pour into a quart-sized glass jar and cool to 110°F/43°C.	**You will first create a mother batch** On the stovetop, heat 1 cup of raw milk to 160°F/71°C, pour into a small glass jar and cool to 110°F/43°C.
Add ½ teaspoon starter cultures. Stir well and set in yogurt maker/incubation chamber for 5 hours.	Add 1/8 teaspoon starter cultures. Stir well and set in yogurt maker/incubation chamber for 4 hours.
Check every ½ hour until set, then cool at room temperature 2 hours before consuming or refrigerating.	Check every ½ hour until set, then cool at room temperature 2 hours before storing in the refrigerator.
Reserve ¼ cup of yogurt to start a new batch (backslopping); do not wait longer than 7 days to start a new batch.	You will not eat this yogurt—it will be the starter for raw milk yogurt. Prepare a new mother batch within 7 days of this first.
For Subsequent Batches	*For Subsequent Batches*
On the stovetop, heat 4 cups of milk to 160°F/71°C, pour into a quart-sized glass jar and cool to 110°F/43°C.	Pour 4 cups of raw milk into a clean, quart-sized glass jar and heat in the yogurt maker/incubation chamber to 110°F/43°C.
Add ¼ cup of yogurt from the previous batch, stir well, cover and cinch with a paper towel and set in yogurt maker/incubation chamber for 5 to 8 hours.	Add 2 tablespoons of the mother batch, stir well, cover and cinch with a paper towel, and keep in the yogurt maker/incubation chamber for 5 to 8 hours.
Once culturing is complete, cool at room temperature for 2 hours before consuming or storing in the refrigerator.	Once culturing is complete, cool at room temperature for 2 hours before consuming or storing in the refrigerator.
Reserve ¼ cup of yogurt to start a new batch (backslopping); do not wait longer than 7 days to start a new batch.	Enjoy all of each batch of yogurt. **But you will need to reserve at least 1 tablespoon of the mother batch, and create a new mother batch by day 7.**

Raw milk yogurt can become quite thin from the inherent enzymes and bacteria of the milk. While this may be fine for smoothies or to drink, it is not the best for serving with a spoon.

How to Flavor and Thicken Yogurt

Homemade yogurt adorned with fresh blueberries and maple syrup

Most of us think of yogurt as a sweet, dessert-like food to enjoy as a snack, or as part of a bigger breakfast. It certainly lends itself to such uses—the tartness of yogurt is a great counterpoint to fruits and sweeteners. But yogurt can be a great savory food, too. Below are some ideas on how to use this delicious and nutritious homemade food.

IF YOU WOULD LIKE TO THICKEN YOUR YOGURT, THERE ARE MANY OPTIONS

- Add more cream or half-and-half to the milk, which will naturally increase the thickness. Just be sure they are not ultra-pasteurized.

- You can strain the finished yogurt by placing it in a few layers of cheesecloth, cinching and allowing the liquid portion (whey) to drain out. Be sure to place the colander over a bowl to collect any of the drained whey, which is very nutritious.

- Heating the milk to a gentle simmer for a few minutes will change the protein structure of the milk, and will create a thicker yogurt (this method works great if you are not wanting to maintain the enzymes and bacteria of raw milk.)

- You can use thickeners, though these are best used with a mother batch technique, as subsequent batches of backslopped cultures will be hampered and degraded by the presence of other ingredients. Although there are other methods, the following are those that are generally safe bets for most from a nutrition and wellness perspective.

THICKENERS

Tapioca Starch

Dissolve 2 tablespoons in a little milk and stir well into the warmed milk before culturing.

Gelatin

Dissolve a teaspoon of gelatin into the milk as it approaches the 110°F/43°C mark. Once the yogurt has set *and has been refrigerated,* it will have a firmer consistency. This firmness will not be present until refrigerated.

FLAVOR IT WITH FRESH OR FROZEN FRUIT, AS WELL AS FRUIT PRESERVES
- Add a teaspoon of vanilla extract to a cup of yogurt, and slice in half of a banana
- Blend in fresh or frozen berries and drizzle with a little raw honey or grade B maple syrup, or a sprinkle of stevia if avoiding sugar
- Stir in a teaspoon or so of fruit preserves to a cup of freshly-made yogurt (fig jam is an excellent choice!)
- Add a ¼ cup of apple or pear sauce and sprinkle with cinnamon and nutmeg
- Stir a ¼ teaspoon cinnamon, ¼ cup raisins and ¼ cup crispy walnuts into a ½ cup of

yogurt, and use as a delicious topping to hot oatmeal

USE IT AS A BASE FOR INCREDIBLY FRESH SALAD DRESSINGS

BASIC DRESSING

This dressing can go any number of directions, based on the herbs and seasonings that are included. Here is the basic recipe for about 1 cup of dressing:

- ½ cup Yogurt
- ¼ cup Extra Virgin Olive Oil
- 4-6 tablespoons' Vinegar or tart Citrus Juice of your choice—suggestions below based on other herbs and seasonings
- 2 tablespoons' filtered Water
- ½ teaspoon Sea Salt, or to taste

Add yogurt, vinegar or juice, and the water to a blender or food processor. Begin blending on a low speed, and drizzle in the olive oil, slowly. Next add the salt, herbs and other seasonings and blend for 20-30 seconds. Serve immediately on the salad of your choice, or store in a glass container in the refrigerator for up to three days. If the dressing is stored, shake well to redistribute all of the ingredients before serving.

While most of us think of yogurt as a sweet delight, it can also be an excellent base for savory dressings and dips.

GARLIC-PESTO STYLE

To the basic recipe above, add:

- 1-2 cloves finely chopped Garlic
- 3-4 leaves fresh Basil, thinly sliced
- 2-3 tablespoons' Balsamic Vinegar
- 2-3 tablespoons' fresh Lemon Juice
- Dash of Red Pepper Flakes, if you choose
- ¼ cup freshly grated Parmesan cheese, if you choose
- 4-5 Crispy Walnuts or 2 tablespoons Crispy Pine Nuts, if you choose

Add the vinegar and juice to the water and yogurt, blend, then drizzle in the olive oil. Add the remainder of the ingredients and blend again to incorporate.

This is lovely over arugula with heirloom tomatoes and fresh mozzarella. It's also a delicious alternative to mayonnaise as a spread, or a base for chicken or tuna salad.

PROVENCE STYLE

In this recipe, decrease the olive oil by half and to the basic recipe above, add:

- ¼ cup toasted Walnut Oil
- ¼ teaspoon dried Savory
- ¼ teaspoon dried Rosemary
- ¼ teaspoon dried Thyme
- ¼ teaspoon dried Oregano
- ¼ teaspoon dried Basil
- ¼ teaspoon dried Fennel Seed
- ¼ teaspoon dried Marjoram
- 2-3 tablespoons' White Wine Vinegar
- 2-3 tablespoons' White Balsamic Vinegar

After blending the yogurt with the water and vinegars, drizzle in the olive oil and walnut oil. Next, sprinkle in the herbs. Because the herbs are dried, allow the mixture to sit at room temperature for a couple of hours before serving, or for overnight in the refrigerator.

This is a delightful dressing on butter lettuce with grilled chicken or poached salmon.

RANCH-STYLE

In this recipe, decrease the yogurt by half and add ¼ cup of organic, full-fat sour cream.

- ¾ teaspoon Garlic Powder
- ¾ teaspoon dried Dill
- 2 teaspoons dried Parsley
- 1 teaspoon Onion Powder
- 2 twists of freshly-ground Black Pepper
- 2-3 tablespoons' White Wine Vinegar (or white balsamic for a sweeter profile)
- 2-3 tablespoons' Raw Apple Cider Vinegar
- 1-2 additional tablespoons' filtered Water, as needed to thin to proper consistency

After blending the yogurt with the sour cream, water and vinegars, drizzle in the olive oil, then add the additional ingredients.

This makes an excellent dip for a crudité platter, as a spread on a roasted turkey and provolone sandwich, or over fresh romaine hearts, cherry tomatoes and Crispy pumpkin seeds.

A little bit of whey and a lot of yogurt

SOME USES FOR WHEY

The liquid portion of yogurt—what many of us pour off when consuming store-bought yogurt—is actually a very nutritious food in its own right.

Fresh whey is a byproduct of cultured dairy. It is the watery portion in cheese-making, what drips off as the milk curds are drained and pressed together to make cheese. It also forms in other cultured dairy foods, such as when yogurt or kefir are left to culture a little too long, and the milk solids combine, leaving the watery portion of milk to separate out.

As long as whey is not heated above 105°F/40.5°C, it is a rich source of digestion-supporting enzymes, beneficial bacteria, bio-available minerals, proteins, and vitamins. It also contains lactose, so any person looking to avoid lactose should probably avoid it.

However, if this is not a concern for you, then here are some ways to incorporate this incredibly nutritious food into your diet.

If stored in the refrigerator in clean, glass jars, whey will keep up to six months. It also freezes well, but there may be some degradation to the beneficial bacteria content.

DRINK IT AS-IS
Whey has a slightly salty, mineral flavor, and is generally a little bit tart. It makes a refreshing beverage to consume after strenuous exercise or on a hot summer's day. Simply pour over ice (or, as Traditional Chinese Medical—TCM--theory would prescribe, enjoy at room temperature to not put additional strain on the digestive system. TCM also recognizes its salty, tart flavor profile as helping to preserve a person's fluids so they're not lost through sweating.) Feel free to add a splash of mineral water or water kefir for some carbonation, if you choose, and a twist of lemon or lime.

USE AS A BASE FOR SMOOTHIES
When blended with fresh or frozen organic berries, a banana, a tablespoon of coconut oil, and a few crispy nuts (see *Dehydrating Nuts and Seeds*), whey becomes the base for a protein-rich, enzyme-potent, nutritious meal or snack.

AS A MEAT TENDERIZER
The enzymes in fresh whey work terrifically to help tenderize thinner slices or chunks of meat, helping to make the more fibrous, less-costly cuts of meat fork-tender. For every pound of meat, use about ½ cup of whey in your marinade. Marinate overnight, or for a full day, in the refrigerator. Drain off and prepare as usual.

TO START OTHER CULTURED FOODS
Fresh, unheated whey is full of lactobacillus bacteria, making it a great culture starter for fermented vegetables. Add a ½ cup to the vegetables as they are being prepared. (No need to add other starters like water kefir if using this method. Simply use it in lieu of the water kefir, and salt as usual.) This method only works with raw whey—such as from milk kefir or yogurt, or in the making of raw cheese.

KEEPING BEANS A PROTEIN-RICH FOOD

Pinto beans, soaked and fermenting before sprouting

Beans are such a versatile and delicious food, an inexpensive vegetarian source of protein…right? Well, as was explained in Dr. Jack Tips' book, *The Pro-Vita Plan*, master herbalist Doc Wheelwright espoused the proper preparation and cooking of legumes to keep them a rich source of protein and other nutrients, a method that is not employed by large-scale food production. The rush to get a lot of food out to the masses, in as little time possible, has left us holding the bag, nutritionally.

WHY YOU SHOULD PREPARE YOUR BEANS THIS WAY

Beans have a rather notorious reputation of being the "magical fruit—the more you eat, the more you toot!" The gassiness one often feels after a serving of beans is the result of our digestive system's inability to break down the large chain carbohydrates known as *oligosaccharides*. When we consume these types of carbohydrates, they pass through our digestive systems largely unchanged…until they reach our bacteria-rich lower intestine. It is here these complex sugars are finally broken down by our intestinal bacteria, generating large quantities of gas in the process. In this scenario, beans then become a food that we don't receive much nutrition from, all the while creating a lot of gas and abdominal bloating and pain in the process. Sounds like something to best be avoided!

It is because of this very well known scenario that it is vitally important to soak beans before consumption. But even beyond this concern, there are other reasons. Just as with grains, nuts and seeds, beans contain various anti-nutrients. From lectin's sticky qualities that can bind to the villi of the small intestine, leading to digestive difficulties; to tannin's mineral-binding activities and interruption of digestive enzyme activity; to phytic acid's mineral-binding actions, anti-nutrients are components common to many foods that we should do our best to minimize. Our ancestors learned that soaking, fermenting and sprouting could improve the digestibility and nutrition of many foods, long-before science isolated and named these minute parts. Allowing water, time and beneficial bacteria to pre-digest our foods, followed by the additional transformation of sprouting, means that we don't need to rely so heavily on our own digestive powers (and the gas that can ensue if a food meets our large intestine's flora basically whole), making for a much more bioavailable food. Unfortunately, commercial food production rarely considers these steps when manufacturing the prepared, convenience foods we purchase. Just one more reason to make your foods from scratch!

Even when beans are soaked before cooking, they are rarely fermented and sprouted. Beans that have been sprouted will have a proportionately greater percentage of protein than beans not sprouted, as complex carbohydrates convert to fiber and starches are washed out. Given that beans are a food many use as a protein source—but which is also a rich source of carbohydrates—this extra step can further tip this food to being a more powerful protein source, and less starchy.

Overcooking any food can be detrimental to its nutrition, and beans are no exception. Delicate amino acids and many B vitamins that are generated in the fermenting and sprouting processes are two easy targets for destruction when foods are overcooked. However, if fermented and sprouted beans are cooked at a barely perceptible simmer, they maintain much of their rich nutritional composition and are in turn a good source of vegetable protein.

HOW WE ENJOY BEANS PREPARED LIKE THIS IN OUR KITCHEN

At home, we enjoy beans prepared this way on salads, in sprouted corn tortillas topped with raw cheese and avocado, and blended into various pastes–beans are just so versatile. And when they're prepared in this manner, they make a great vegetarian source of protein in a given meal. It should be mentioned that they have a firmer texture, making them more filling as well.

On the left, a soaked pinto bean about to sprout, on the right, a dried pinto bean

PREPARATION OF PROTEIN-RICH BEANS

Pinto beans that have been soaked and sprouting—perfect!

MAKES APPROXIMATELY 2 CUPS OF PREPARED BEANS

- 1 cup of organic, rinsed and sorted whole Beans
- 2-3 cups of warm Water, in the 110°F/43°C range
- 3-4 tablespoons of fresh Water Kefir (this isn't mandatory, but it will hasten the mild fermentation process)
- Any Vegetables and Seasonings you would like for your broth

Soak the beans in warm water and water kefir (if using), for at least 8 hours, kept at room temperature, in a large, loosely covered bowl (a bound paper towel works great.) If you're not using the water kefir as a fermentation starter, then try to keep the soaking bowl in a warm spot, to allow the wild fermentation to occur more quickly. In this instance, keeping the bowl in the microwave (turned off!) with a couple of bottles of hot water can create and maintain a warm, stable temperature. Make sure the beans stay under water—if they plump up and break the surface of the water, simply pour on a little more warmed water to cover.

Beans after eight hours of soaking should be pliable to the teeth, no longer crunchy. You should also see little bubbles of fermentation when you move the bowl. If not, stir from the bottom to break up any surface molds and soak for a few more hours.

When ready, drain and rinse the beans, then spread them in a colander, keeping them level throughout, and loosely the top of the colander with a paper towel. Place the covered colander inside a large bowl. (Placing the beans in a colander keeps air circulating on more of their surface area, and makes for easy rinsing until they begin to sprout.) Keep beans at room temperature, checking every few hours for a small, white sprout to appear. Rinse every 4-5 hours until sprouts have appeared.

Once the beans have just sprouted, prepare your cooking water in a large stockpot. Plan to have at least 6-8 cups of water or liquid for cooking. This might be bone broth, or simply water in which vegetables and seasonings of your choice have been cooked. Add the beans and bring back up to just a visible simmer. Maintain at this heat for 40-50 minutes, or until the beans have softened through, but have more texture than the commonly prepared "mushy" bean.

Serve immediately as-is, or puree in a food processor for a delicious bean dip, or as a rich spread for sandwiches and wraps.

OTHER CONSIDERATIONS

- Sprouted kidney and cannellini beans are incredibly toxic unless cooked well. We just avoid them.

- Make sure your beans never develop slime, mold or take on an off odor while sprouting—if they do, discard them and start over. The scent of the beans may be stronger as they are sprouting, but it should still smell like the bean and not something else. Keep them well covered with water when soaking, and rinsed well when sprouting.

Giving a brief fold to soaked and fermented Water Kefir Bread dough before placing in the Dutch oven

SOAKING AND FERMENTING GRAINS

All grains can and should be soaked—in this picture, quinoa flakes are being prepared for cooking

Grains are a staple food in diets around the globe. Their durability and long storage life lend them to being safeguards against famines, making them the cornerstone of the rise of various empires throughout history. However, it is this same durability that can be a very significant hindrance to digestion if there is not first a softening pre-digestion of their rough and bound components. And while humans through the ages have devised various means to extract the nutrition buried in these foods, modern food production techniques have largely overlooked these very crucial steps.

A LITTLE ON THE HISTORY OF SOAKING GRAINS

Like so many of the traditional food preparation techniques, no one can really trace soaking and fermenting grains to a given people. However, it is clear in looking over historical research, that it has long been common for people to go to the trouble of these preparatory steps before cooking and consumption. In parts of Asia, fermented porridges of various legumes and cereals, as well as different flatbreads are consumed regularly, and have been for a millennia, techniques handed down generation to generation. In Africa, soaked and fermented sorghum, corn and millet are traditional staples, served as cakes and porridges. Fermented corn and rice are also important staple foods in many Latin American countries. In Europe and North America, there is the age-old tradition of making sourdough bread with rye and wheat, a type of food production that continues to this day.

WHY YOU SHOULD SOAK AND FERMENT YOUR OWN GRAINS

In her seminal book on traditional foods, *Nourishing Traditions,* author Sally Fallon shared research findings regarding a common anti-nutrient in all grains, phytic acid. In fact, phytic acid is but one of a number of different anti-nutrients that are in grains. These components have been likened to Mother Nature's insecticide, possibly an attempt to keep predators (humans and other grain-consuming animals) from eating too much of them. When consumed in large amounts, digestive distress and other issues can ensue from their consumption. In the case of phytic acid, it binds tightly to the bran of grains (and legumes, nuts and seeds as well), and chelates these minerals right out of our bodies, keeping us from absorbing them; it also impairs the digestibility of carbohydrates and proteins. Lectins are another anti-nutrient that have been implicated in many concerns, from nutritional deficiencies to allergic reactions to digestive impairment. Tannins are another common anti-nutrient, a class of polyphenols that binds to minerals, inactivates digestive enzymes and reduces the bioavailability of protein.

It should come as no surprise that regular consumption of foods rich in these anti-nutrients can eventually lead to significant nutritional deficiencies. In some respects, eating whole grains, in unsoaked and unfermented form, is actually more detrimental than consuming refined, "white" grains—it is in the bran that these anti-nutrients are found.

However, one can keep the incredible nutrition in these foods, by simply employing the ancient practices of soaking and fermentation.

HOW WE SOAK AND FERMENT GRAINS IN OUR KITCHEN

No matter what grain I'm using—whether it's rice or oats or spelt or even a grain-like seed such as quinoa—I always soak the grains in a warm, slightly acidic "bath." I allow at least 15 hours, but usually closer to 24, for soaking. What cues me to its completion is either the presence of bubbles in the water (a sign of lacto-fermentation), and/or the wonderful, tart scent of fermentation (with grains, this can take on the scent of sourdough.) Once one of these two signs is present, then I'll proceed onto the next steps of rinsing and cooking. Being patient with the process allows gentle heat, water and beneficial bacteria to break down not only the afore-mentioned anti-nutrients, but also to predigest some of the complex carbohydrates into simpler sugars. And the end result is a hot cereal or whole, steamed grain that has a slightly tangy flavor, not unlike a mild sourdough. It tastes wonderful, and it moves well through the belly, not sitting heavily in the gut.

Part of the soaking medium I use is water kefir. I like this because many of the other beneficial bacteria-rich soaking suggestions—yogurt, fresh whey, kefir—are full of calcium. And while this is a great boon in many respects, when it comes to trying to break down anti-nutrients, there is research showing it may actually impede this effort. So, rather than take a chance, I use water kefir. Another option is to allow wild fermentation to occur, simply from the inherent bacteria on the organic, non-irradiated grains. Just be certain to use de-chlorinated water if you go this route, as chlorine kills bacteria…even the good ones!

Brown rice, soaking and mildly fermenting before cooking

SOAKED AND FERMENTED WHOLE GRAINS

On the left, whole, dried brown rice; on the right, the same rice, soaked and gently fermented and ready to cook

MAKES APPROXIMATELY 2 CUPS OF COOKED GRAINS

- 1 cup of organic Grains, rinsed well (Most any grain will do, but if using a large-kernel grain such as spelt or kamut, you may want to coarsely grind the grain to expose more surface area. A grain mill or milling attachment to a food processor is best, but a few spins in a coffee grinder will work as well.)
- 2-3 cups warm, filtered Water (in the 110°F/43°C range)
- 3-4 tablespoons Water Kefir (not mandatory, but helps to prepare the water for culturing more quickly, predigesting the carbohydrates)

Place grains and warm water in a glass or ceramic bowl, and mix in the water kefir. Cover loosely with a bound paper towel, to keep dust and insects out. Place in a warm, undisturbed spot for at least 12 hours. Make sure the grains stay under the water; fermentation is an anaerobic activity, so if the grains plump up and break the water's surface, simply add a little more warm water to cover completely. (I like to use our yogurt maker as an incubator. Just remove the lid and place the glass or ceramic bowl so that it nestles in the rim of the yogurt maker. Then cover the bowl, drape with a towel for even insulation, turn on the yogurt maker and leave it overnight. This temperature is warm enough to allow more activity from the lacto-fermentation, hastening the fermentation process.)

Placing the grains in a glass bowl, covered with a tea towel, onto the powered yogurt maker for a warm soaking

After 12-15 hours, stir the grains from the bottom. If you notice the tart scent of fermentation and see bubbles rising through the water, then you know the beneficial bacteria are proliferating. If not, stir again to break up any dust or microscopic surface molds, and check back in a few hours. Making certain the temperature is warm enough for fermentation to occur will help—if it's less than about 70°F/21°C, you might move your bowl to a warmer locale. A microwave or oven with a couple bottles of hot water can be a warm, stable environment that encourages beneficial bacteria activity.

Once ready, you can either cook the grains in their soaking water (easiest to do with oatmeal), or rinse them and start with either fresh water or broth. In either case, just have hot water on hand to add to the grains as they cook, should you need it; plan to start with enough liquid to cover your soaked grains by about ¼ inch. Remember, the grains are really much closer to completion than grains cooked from the dry state, so expect a shorter cooking time. A rule of thumb is about 10-15 minutes less cooking time than cooking grains from a raw, dry state.

Place the grains and their cooking liquid into a medium-sized pot and bring to a boil over medium heat. Season with a pinch of sea salt and any other spices you choose. Once gently boiling, stir the grains, cover and reduce the heat to a very low simmer. Check for doneness every few minutes.

SOME CONSIDERATIONS

• Oats cook very quickly, and their hydrophilic nature requires more water than other grains. Plan to have hot water on hand to add in as they cook.

• Quinoa also cooks quite quickly, and it will likely sprout during the soaking process. Amaranth is similar. This is fine and simply enhances digestibility.

• Rice, spelt, kamut and other large-sized grains take longer to cook, generally. Be patient with these—while other grains may be ready as soon as 5 to 10 minutes, these larger grains may take closer to a half hour or so.

Does it get much better than homemade bread?

WATER KEFIR BREAD

Crusty and hearty water kefir bread, fresh from the oven and ready for slicing

This bread has become a staple in our home. With the grain mill, I am able to rotate through using different flours, but always working with the same basic ingredients—a gluten-bearing ancient grain (Einkorn, Emmer, Rye, Spelt or Kamut), fresh water kefir, sea salt and warm water. That's it—no yeast (beyond the inherent yeast in the water kefir), no leavening agents like baking powder or soda; just those simple ingredients, and a 24-hour fermentation period. I grind the flour to a medium coarseness, so, if you're looking to use store-bought flour, use a medium grind if you can find it to keep the ratios the same.

Using the grain mill to make fresh flour

Do try your hand at different types of gluten-bearing grains (this recipe is not for someone avoiding gluten!) as you work with this basic recipe. Some versions may come out a little "wetter" than others after the fermentation stage, but with a quick dusting of flour on the outside of the dough, plus the searing that happens by being poured into the hot Dutch oven, I've yet to have a loaf of any variety come out anything but delicious!

This bread does not make a particularly high loaf, but it is excellent all the same. It has a terrific crust all around, is mildly tart like sourdough, and is soft on the inside. It reheats really well in the toaster and tastes like a dream with fresh butter!

MAKES 1 LOAF, APPROXIMATELY 7"x10" OVAL
- 2 ¼ cups medium-grind Einkorn Flour, sifted
- 2 ¼ cups medium-grind Emmer Flour, sifted
- 3 teaspoons Celtic Sea Salt
- 1 ½ cups warm, filtered Water

- 1 ½ cups fresh Water Kefir
- Butter for greasing the fermenting bowl
- Extra flour for dusting a second glass bowl
- Medium-sized Dutch Oven (or some other heavy-duty, lidded casserole dish or roasting pan) for baking

METHOD

In a large mixing bowl, combine flours and stir in the sea salt. Pour in the warm water and the water kefir, and mix well to saturate the flour. Grease a large, glass mixing bowl, and pour in the dough. Cover with a lid and set in a warm area and do not disturb for 24 hours. (To keep a nice, even heat, I use our yogurt maker. Remove the lid from the yogurt maker and set the bowl at the top of the unit. Turn on the yogurt maker, cover the bowl and place a towel around it to help keep the heat evenly dispersed—see the photos on page 116 for illustration.)

Coconut oil for greasing the bowl for rising and the coarseness of the freshly ground flour

In a few simple steps, the flour is mixed with the water kefir, warm water and salt. It is then placed in the bowl greased with oil and set in a warm spot—in this instance, on top of the yogurt maker.

At the end of the 24 hours, the dough should have risen rather significantly—you should see air pockets throughout the dough as you look at it through the bowl. It should also have a pleasantly tart scent. The rising and the tart odor are indicative of lacto-fermentation—the bacteria and the yeasts in the water kefir have been busy predigesting the dough for you!

After many hours and a warm temperature, the air pockets of fermentation in the dough, created by the carbon dioxide being generated as the beneficial bacteria and yeasts of the water kefir consume and transform the carbohydrates of the flour.

After the soaking and fermentation is complete, it is time to bake. Place the Dutch oven on the middle rack of your oven, and set at 425°F/218°C. Allow it heat in the oven for at least 30 minutes. Dust a large, glass mixing bowl with fresh flour and fold in the dough. Lightly dust the top of the dough with additional flour, and fold the dough once or twice with your hands. Allow it to rest for 30-45 minutes while the oven and Dutch oven heat. Once the Dutch oven has pre-heated for at least 30 minutes, remove it and take off the lid, and pour in the floured dough, which will sizzle as it hits the bottom of the pan. Cover quickly and place it back in the oven.

Pouring the fermented dough into a fresh glass bowl, dusted with flour and sprinkled with a little flour from the top.

 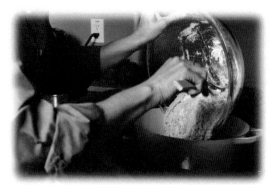

Giving the dough a little fold-over a couple of times before allowing to rest a little longer before baking. Pouring the dough into the preheated Dutch oven for baking.

Carefully removing the bread from the oven—very hot!

After 30 minutes, remove the lid from the Dutch oven. Keep baking for an additional 10-15 minutes, then remove it from the oven. Flip the Dutch oven over a dish, and the bread should fall directly onto it. Transfer the loaf to rest on a stainless steel trivet, allowing it to cool for 10 minutes before slicing. Store in parchment or waxed paper at room temperature for up to 3 days. Also stores well in the refrigerator and can be frozen for up to 3 months if stored in a freezer-safe bag.

A slice of delicious water kefir bread with cultured butter

Soaked and gently fermented walnuts

SOAKING NUTS AND SEEDS...AND MAKING THEM CRISPY AGAIN!

Raw, organic pumpkin seeds that have been soaked, mildly fermented, and are now ready for dehydration

Raw nuts and seeds are delicious foods, straight from nature's bounty, ready for our snacking delight. Well, almost ready. As with grains and legumes, nuts and seeds do have various anti-nutrients that actually block our absorption of much of their good nutrition, so some preparation is needed to get the most from these foods. This technique, coined "Crispy Nuts" by Sally Fallon in *Nourishing Traditions*, is a terrific way to soak away those anti-nutrients...then bring them back to crunchy goodness with a dehydrator or low setting on your oven.

131

A LITTLE ON THE HISTORY OF SOAKING NUTS AND SEEDS

Fallon cites the Aztecs and their preparation of *pepitas* (pumpkin seeds), by soaking them in salt water and drying them in the sun, as an ancient practice she emulates with her methods. And, as with other traditional food preparation techniques, this is a practice that has been handed down through the generations. Who first thought to do this step? We will likely never know, but soaking (and in my recipe, waiting for a little fermentation to occur), is very much in keeping with the natural process of a nut or seed germinating. When warm, moist, enzymatically-rich components come together, the vitality of the raw nut or seed is unleashed, and the anti-nutrients of tannins, phytic acid, lectins are broken down.

The bubbles of fermentation, atop pumpkin seeds that have been soaking overnight in sea salt and water kefir

WHY YOU SHOULD SOAK YOUR NUTS AND SEEDS

As mentioned, the right conditions lend themselves to a breakdown of these very real anti-nutrients. Warm water, time and mild fermentation break down the mineral-binding action of phytic acid, the sticky qualities of lectins and the enzymatic-disruption of tannins. What is left in the wake of an overnight soaking is an enzymatically-rich food that is much easier to digest, delivering on all the nutrition that is in those nuts and seeds.

HOW WE USE CRISPY NUTS IN OUR KITCHEN

One of my first traditional kitchen purchases was a dehydrator...and I've never regretted the investment. It has allowed me to dehydrate fruits and vegetables to enjoy long past their growing season, to make jerky from wild-caught salmon and pastured beef, to preserve fresh herbs, and to dehydrate soaked nuts and seeds, while maintaining their enzymatic activity. While you can certainly use an oven, set on its lowest temperature (usually 150°F/65.5°C), this low heat is still too high to maintain enzymes. However, a dehydrator, set at 105°F/40.5°C, will produce a crispy nut or seed that is not only delicious, more bioavailable and easier to digest than a raw nut, but it will also still contain enzymes that further enhance digestion. And, given that most dehydrators are available in the $100-range, it is a sound investment that doesn't put too much of a dent in the pocketbook.

Once the nuts and seeds are dehydrated, store them in glass jars in the refrigerator, where they wait to be enjoyed any number of ways:

• As the protein component of a sweet or savory trail mix
• Tossed on top of a salad
• Blended with other nuts, sweeteners and oils to make snack bars
• Mixed into a smoothie
• Enjoyed as-is, maybe with some fresh fruit
Just beware--the mild saltiness they take on from the salt water soaking is very addictive!

As with the other recipes for preparing beans and grains, I like to use water kefir as a starter culture in the soaking water. However, this is not mandatory. If you're working with good, organic, non-irradiated raw nuts and seeds, there should be enough inherent bacteria on the seeds for wild fermentation to occur. Just be sure to use de-chlorinated, filtered water—the chlorine will kill all bacteria, even the good ones!

From left to right, a raw walnut, a soaked walnut and a dehydrated walnut

BASIC RECIPE FOR SOAKING, FERMENTING AND DRYING NUTS AND SEEDS
MAKES APPROXIMATELY 2 CUPS OF NUTS OR SEEDS

- 2 cups of shelled, organic, raw Nuts (Filberts, Almonds, Walnut halves, Hazelnuts, Pecan halves, Macadamia Nuts, Peanuts, Pine Nuts) or Seeds (Pepitas/Pumpkin Seeds, Sunflower Seeds, Winter Squash Seeds), rinsed

- 1 tablespoon Sea Salt, dissolved in 3 cups filtered, warm water (110°F/43°C range)

- 2-3 tablespoons of Water Kefir (optional)

Place rinsed nuts or seeds in a glass quart jar and pour in the salted water. Stir well and add in the water kefir, if you choose to use it. Cinch the jar with a cloth or paper towel and rubber band and place in a warm, undisturbed spot overnight, or at 6-7 hours. Make certain all the nuts or seeds stay in the water; if they plump up and break the water's surface, simply add a little more warm water to cover.

At the end of this time, you may notice a few bubbles of fermentation as you tip the jar, or stir the ingredients, especially if you did prime the water with the active cultures, and/or if the temperature was at least 70°F/21°C during the soaking period. This fermentation is just one more sign of pre-digestion of the nuts and seeds.

Drain the nuts or seeds with a fine meshed colander and give a quick rinse with fresh water. You can now store the nuts or seeds as-is in a clean glass jar in the refrigerator—they are very nutritious this way, just moist. If you choose to stop at this step, be sure to rinse them at least every other day, keep them refrigerated, and plan to consume them within a week.

Soaked and fermented pumpkin seeds are drained and rinsed with clean water before storing in the refrigerator in a clean jar, or dehydrated for crispiness and longer keeping.

IF YOU CHOOSE TO DEHYDRATE THEM AND MAKE THEM CRISPY, YOU CAN USE ONE OF THE TWO FOLLOWING OPTIONS:

- **Option 1.** *This requires only an oven, but likely at the cost of enzymatic vitality of the* *finished nuts or seeds.* Spread all the nuts or seeds evenly over a cookie sheet and place in an oven at its lowest setting (hopefully 150°F/65.5°C or lower.) Keep in the oven for at least 12 hours, possibly up to 24. Stir them occasionally and check them for crunchiness and dryness. When completely dry, set the tray out at room temperature to cool. Transfer to a glass or ceramic jar for storage, and cover tightly; stores well in the refrigerator up to 6 months.

- **Option 2.** *This requires a dehydrator with a low-heat setting, which will maintain the enzymatic vitality of the finished nuts or seeds.* Spread all the nuts or seeds evenly over dehydrator trays, and set at 105°F/40.5°C. Leave overnight, or at least 12 hours. If nuts or seeds are still moist, keep checking every 6 hours or so, until completely dry and crunchy. Once complete, allow nuts or seeds to cool to room temperature, then transfer to a clean glass or ceramic jar for storage, and cover tightly; stores well in the refrigerator for up to 6 months.

Smoothing out the pumpkin seeds in the dehydrator tray for even drying

LET FOOD BE THY MEDICINE AND MEDICINE BE THY FOOD.
HIPPOCRATES

LIFE EXPECTANCY WOULD GROW BY LEAPS AND BOUNDS IF VEGETABLES
SMELLED AS GOOD AS BACON.
DOUG LARSON

RESOURCES

For an extensive listing of the healthiest foods in supermarkets, natural food stores, and by mail order, contact the **Weston A. Price Foundation** for a copy of their Annual Shopping Guide. Products are listed as Good and Best, with recommendations of which foods to avoid. It is a small investment at $2-3 per booklet.

Per their website, The Weston A. Price Foundation is "dedicated to restoring nutrient-dense foods to the human diet through education, research and activism. It supports a number of movements that contribute to this objective including accurate nutrition instruction, organic and biodynamic farming, pasture-feeding of livestock, community-supported farms, honest and informative labeling, prepared parenting and nurturing therapies." They are a tax-exempt charity organization, and their website is brimming with health-related articles and support to help people locate more nutritious foods in their area. They also have local chapters throughout the world, where you can connect with people in your area who support the efforts of the Foundation.

THE WESTON A. PRICE FOUNDATION
PMB 106-380
4200 Wisconsin Avenue, NW
Washington, DC 20016 USA
Phone: (202) 363-4394
www.westonaprice.org

To locate a Natural Foods' Store, Community Supported Agriculture (CSA) program and Buying Clubs near you, contact **Green People**.

THE GREENPEOPLE TEAM
300 Georgia St., Suite #1
Hollywood, FL 33019
Phone: (401) eco-biz4 (326-2494)
www.greenpeople.org.

To locate a Natural Foods' Cooperative in your area, contact the **Coop Directory Service**.

COOP DIRECTORY SERVICE
1254 Etna Street, St. Paul, MN 55106
Phone and Fax: 651-774-9189
E-mail address: thegang@coopdirectory.org
www.coopdirectory.org

For an excellent selection of various yogurt, kefir, water kefir, cheese, sourdough and other types of culture starters, contact **Cultures for Health**.
They also have dehydrators, basic grain mills, yogurt makers and all the tools needed for making cultured foods at home. Their support with free video tutorials and written instructions is unsurpassed, and they have a wonderful customer support team.

CULTURES FOR HEALTH
807 N. Helen Avenue
Sioux Falls, SD 57104
Phone: 800-962-1959
www.culturesforhealth.com

YEMOOS is another great source for culture starters, both fresh and dehydrated. They are strictly online.
Visit www.yemoos.com.

To learn more about the importance of eating animal foods from animals reared in their natural environments, with a directory of US, Canadian and International farms and ranches, contact **Eat Wild.**

EAT WILD STORE
Mailing Address
PO Box 7321
Tacoma, WA 98417
Phone: 866-453-8489 Toll-Free (US Only) from outside US 1-253-759-2318
www.eatwild.com

To learn more about the nutrition and benefits of raw milk and how to find raw milk in your area, contact **The Campaign for Real Milk**, a project of the Weston A. Price Foundation.

THE CAMPAIGN FOR REAL MILK
The Weston A. Price Foundation
PMB 106-3804200 Wisconsin Ave., NW
Washington, DC 20016 USA
Phone: (202) 363-4394
For questions or general information about raw milk or the Weston A. Price Foundation: info@westonaprice.org
www.realmilk.com

Please stay in touch—I would love to hear from you! Share your triumphs in the kitchen, ask me questions if you find yourself stymied on a technique, or divulge a favorite recipe. Email me at sarica@naturallylivingtoday.com, or contact me via my blog, www.naturallylivingtoday.com, where I share thoughts and recipes for living more naturally and vibrantly in the modern world.

GLOSSARY
GLOSSARY

Made in the USA
Charleston, SC
06 September 2013